Rhythms
of the HEART

Rhythms of the HEART

Embracing Life After Death

Debra Lee Tucker

T HOUSE PUBLISHING

T House Publishing, LLC

ISBN 978-1-4507-3927-6

Library of Congress number pending

Published by: T House Publishing, LLC
Cover and interior design: Rick Tucker

Inquiries about *Rhythms of the Heart*, email: rhythmsoftheheart10@gmail.com

Printed in the United States of America

DEDICATION

To my precious family–

Rick: My husband, confidante and ultimate example of loyalty and dedication. Thank you for taking our marriage vows seriously – "For better or worse, richer or poorer, in sickness and in health, for as long as you both shall live."

My girls, Abby & April: I can honestly say that I have learned to love in ways that I never thought would be possible – unconditionally, unselfishly and without regret. Being your mother has been and continues to be my greatest joy, challenge and fulfillment in this life.

Ella: Your innocence and enthusiasm for life encourages me to continually seek childlike faith. How blessed I am to be your NaNa.

> Oh rhythm of my heart,
>   is beating like a drum
> With the words "I love you"
>   rolling off my tongue.
> No, never will I roam,
>   for I know my place is home,
> Where the ocean meets the sky,
>   I'll be sailing
>
> –Rod Stewart, *Rhythm of My Heart*

THE BLACK ROSE

Black roses do not exist in nature as such, but nevertheless they are often featured in fictional works. The flowers commonly called black roses are actually a very dark red color.

In the 18th century, the language of flowers became popular. In this code, the black rose is a symbol of death, hatred, revenge, sorrow or mourning. It can also be used when conveying a farewell. The black rose's quality of being a rare flower renders it an apt symbol of profound love, or other such things of a rare nature.

It also is the symbol of rebirth, especially referring to beauty or the mind.

TABLE OF CONTENTS

PART THREE

INTRODUCTION

God is a god of order and organization. I love that. I need order and structure in my life to function and feel secure. In my opinion, everything runs smoother when a system is in place and expectations are outlined. The natural rhythms in life provide a continuous cycle of existence and continuity. The breath in our chest rises and falls to the sound of crashing ocean waves on the sand and the slow, constant dripping of spring rain on a tin roof. The arts, as demonstrated in music, poetry and dance provide pace, beat, tempo and time as they energize our spirits and soothe our senses.

But, what happens when a soloist sings a sour note or a piano is out of tune? When a drummer is off beat with the band? A ballerina misses her queue or a poet forgets his lines? You know. You cringe, tighten your shoulders and try not to notice, or at least not let the performer see you notice. You hope they can get back on track and in sync and finish the production. But, it's harder to recover once the rhythm has been broken and everyone involved has been affected.

It's not that I don't like to be spontaneous and break the rules every now and then; it's human nature. Our desire for change and a break in routine challenges us to try new things and entertain new ideas.

Sometimes life feels very ordinary, organized and uneventful. We wake up, get out of bed (happy or not), shower, dress, eat breakfast, drive to work, and perform our outlined duties for the day. After a day of decisions and expectations, we make our way home to our family, have dinner, attend school, church or social commitments, come home and fall into bed, exhausted body, mind and spirit. We do all of this with the expectation of waking the next morning to "do it all again," only altering variations within the day's prearranged commitments. Our routines begin and end as scheduled and often, whether purposely or out of perceived obligation, the busyness manages to distract us from the circumstances we are powerless to change. We begin by telling ourselves that this is a form of survival and self-preservation, but often find that what we end up with is self-destruction.

WHAT "TO DO"?

My life began and ended with an endless, unattainable "to do" list. I actually had a written list each day that I could check off to make myself feel productive. Sometimes, I would add to my list at the end of the day if my performance included "above and beyond" tasks. I often felt that those achievements and accomplishments gave visible, constructive value to my life and an explanation for being on this planet and taking up space and oxygen. There was evidence that God obviously wanted me to be alive and "wasn't done with me yet". I had a performance-based, works mentality that was never good enough for me, or my perception of God's expectations of me.

I have talked to countless people, men and women, who have the same problem. The harder they work, and the more they achieve, the more they are reminded how much more could be done, or at least how it could be improved.

Frustration comes from the inability to accomplish as much as we would like in a 24-hour day, a five-day work-week, a mere 365 days annually or more importantly, a 70-80 year life span. Many suffer from sleeplessness, resulting in chronic fatigue, both mental and physical, job burnout, family tension, and health issues. Lest you think the Christian community has been given immunity to these issues, take a close look at the divorce rate, drug and alcohol addiction statistics and health concerns of the churched population. We are all human.

DON'T WORRY, BE HAPPY

What did I have to worry about? From all outward appearances, our family was living the American dream. I had a wonderful, dedicated husband, employed by one of the largest mission organizations in the nation. He was able to work remotely from home which allowed him time with family. We had two beautiful, healthy, intelligent daughters and a perfect granddaughter.

We enjoyed Christian fellowship and service with other believers in a respected, growing church. We lived in a nice home that we had designed and contracted ourselves. We were totally debt free and lived in a safe, wholesome community. I was employed by an organization where I had been involved for years and was eventually promoted to director, providing me with purpose and fulfillment in the workplace.

So, why was I anxious, angry and unhappy? I didn't know, but on several occasions, I said to my husband, "I can't keep doing this. It's killing me." Even I didn't know what those prophetic words meant as they were spoken from my heart and lips… but God did.

MORE TO LIFE

My life suddenly changed in a moment – no warning, no preparation. The events and days that followed would prove to be life sustaining as well as life changing. As you read the story of my experience, you will see how precious life is and what you can do to embrace every moment.

As you join me on my journey, you will also understand that the rhythms of the heart affect every aspect of life; our minds and emotions as well as our bodies. When we are out of sync with God, our marriages, families, health, emotions, and priorities suffer.

By living a life through everyday choices and by our own design, believing that we can leave God out of the equation, we find that we not only have been climbing the wrong ladder to happiness and success, but it's been leaning again the wrong wall. Eventually, when a life-altering event occurs (and you can be certain that it will), we realize that we have not avoided life's challenges, but traded them for battles within our souls.

PART ONE

Love anything, and your heart will certainly be wrung and possibly broken. If you want to make sure of keeping it intact, you must give your heart to no one, not even to an animal. Wrap it careful round with hobbies and little luxuries; avoid all entanglements; lock it up safe in the casket or coffin of your selfishness. But in that casket–safe, dark, motionless, airless–it will change. It will not be broken; it will become unbreakable, impenetrable, irredeemable.

–C.S. Lewis, *The Four Loves*

Ordinary Days

Wednesday morning started like so many days. It felt very routine and ordinary. I slipped into the coordinated outfit I had laid out in my closet the night before, an ensemble built around the new jade fall leaf necklace my husband Rick had given me just two days earlier to celebrate our twenty-eighth wedding anniversary. It was a gift I was excited to show off.

No real time for breakfast. I could grab something at work before staff meeting or maybe have a cup of coffee before lunch. Either way, eating a meal wasn't a priority. My plate was full: planning meetings, various task agendas, and a hectic schedule. That's just the way I liked it: not enough time to think about one thing for very long.

It wasn't an unusual day as to routines, but the date itself evoked emotion. Twenty-seven years ago at 8 a.m., I had given birth to a healthy, beautiful, 6 pound 3 ounce little girl. Overwhelmed by the wonder of life, I felt Abby was the most precious gift from God I had ever known. She was my first child and I adored her. I had always made it a point to tell both of my children about the day and hours leading up to their deliveries into this world as we celebrated their birthdays – a reminder that our children are a joy and a precious part of our lives.

If I stopped long enough, I was sure I would realize how tired I really was.

Unfortunately, a challenging turn of events over the last three years had stolen the daughter we had known and changed our close, loving relationship to a strained and distant one at best. The birthday reminder was a bittersweet combination of wonderful memories as a young family and an uncertain future.

My reflection in the dimly lit mirror caught my attention as I rushed toward the door. I looked tired. If I stopped long enough, I was sure I would realize how tired I really was. But there was no time for reflection or for slowing down. Neither would be beneficial or productive.

Rick was still catering to my needs as we walked to the garage. "You got lunch? Did you eat breakfast? I put your water bottle in your front seat. Have a great day." I forced a smile and waved, backing out of the garage. As soon as the car cleared the driveway, I rolled my eyes in resentment at the way my husband smothered and hovered over me. Of course, I knew he was being helpful and attentive, but it bugged me that he was always so available and predictable.

I mean, weren't men supposed to be tough and manly, and have a competitive nature, or at least want to kill something and drag it home for dinner? But I was sure most women would love to have a husband who was as sensitive to their needs as mine. *Ugh!* I thought. *I guess we can never be truly happy.* But there was no time to dwell on the negative, especially before I arrived at my high-energy, challenging job as client services director for one of the nation's largest crisis pregnancy centers.

As I drove toward the highway crossroads, I briefly considered taking the interstate. I rarely chose that typical, congested morning drive of sleepy, agitated drivers, especially when there was such a nice alternative. The two-lane back roads provided a fifteen-minute reprieve from the normal rush hour traffic and stress; the picturesque backdrop of Jersey cows and wildflowers was solace for me.

The fall morning was crisp; a haze of frost lay on the windshield. I exhaled the cool air with a prayer of thanksgiving, but somehow felt a heaviness that wouldn't be ignored. I knew I could not get on with the day until I had wished Abby a happy birthday. Rounding the sharp curve at the top of the hill, I had to change hands to maneuver the turn and call her number on the phone. I knew she wouldn't answer, especially at that time of the morning, but I could leave a voice mail. As the line rang on the other end, I considered hitting the red button and rehearsing what I wanted to say before I left the message, but when I heard her voice on the

Twenty-seven years ago today had been one of the most memorable and best days of my life.

recording, I just talked to her from my heart.

I pictured Abby's petite frame and long black hair that sometimes hid her childlike, shy smile. I told her I hoped she had a fantastic birthday and that she should know that 27 years ago today had been one of the most memorable and best days of my life. I told her I loved her more than she could know or comprehend. Her dad and I had a gift for her, I continued, if we could know where she was or how to send it to her. I closed the phone, fighting tears and feeling emotionally drained, but knowing I could never let her birthday pass without telling her I loved her and acknowledging the memorable day. I took a deep breath and hoped the message would have a positive impact on her, but knowing that regardless of her reaction, I had let her know how I felt.

We had always celebrated birthdays in a big way, beginning with Abby's first, and every one after that. When Abby was too young to realize what a birthday party was, we invited people from the office where her father and I worked. They were all in their 20s, without children, and many unmarried, but we were excited to share the event with everyone. We usually celebrated the birthday for at least a week, with various friends and family members and themed cakes and decorations. It was a big deal; we were celebrating life.

Crossing the bridge over Springfield Lake, I observed the swollen water level following the recent flooding of the rivers, creeks, and waterways. Even through the thick fog, I spotted the great blue heron where he was perched on an orange bobbing buoy in the lake. He was there as always, faithfully taking his position to greet commuters and passersby. I often smiled and nodded in his direction as an acknowledgement of and appreciation for his role and participation in life. His dedicated stance was a simple but true example of how God is in the small things. The mundane things we think are not important are often the very things that someone else is counting on to begin their day or get them through a difficult time.

Following the view of the lake, the remainder of the drive was typical traffic lights, congestion and morning rush hour. The parking lot at work was mostly empty except for three cars I recognized. Those occupied spaces told me who the eager beavers and morning people were at the non-profit organization where I worked. Proudly, I secured my usual corner parking space, knowing Rick would be grateful for the likelihood of one less ding on the driver's side door of the Infiniti this week.

I walked to the front door of our stucco building, inhaling my lungs full of fresh, cool air and quickly exhaling the air my lungs had warmed, resulting in a fog that encircled my head like a wreath of smoke. I chuckled at the thought that as a child, my friends and I would pretend we were smoking a cigarette while playing on the playground during early morning recess. We were innocent children imitating adults, long before the harmful affect of tobacco use was revealed.

I tugged to open the heavy glass door, walked to the elevator, pushed the button for the third floor, and waited, holding my lunch bag and purse. I had noticed that the kelly green elevator door didn't really match the lobby's newly updated décor of dove-gray painted walls and dark gray marbled tile. It was evident that shortly after the remodel, words and symbols of heartfelt devotion had already been lightly carved into the wall near the elevator button. Our clients were often young and passionate about their feelings and needed to express them. Ding!

Finally! Patience might be a virtue, but arriving early was a must. I was usually in one of two stages at the elevator: running three to five minutes later than I wanted to be, or 5-10 minutes early, wishing I had spent time on more important things, like my hair. Searching for the elevator keys I could never find unless my entire purse was emptied, I gave up and dropped everything to the floor. Everyone joked about the sluggish antiquated elevator crane. Our staff had nicknamed the green machine Eeyore, after the lovable but painfully slow donkey from Winnie the Pooh.

Eventually the third floor button lit up and I stepped into the reception area of the pregnancy medical clinic. The overhead lights had yet to be turned on so I flipped the switch. I briefly greeted a staff member as we both headed toward the kitchen to brew a cup of coffee. Our quaint staff break and lunch area featured a regular-size 12-cup coffee maker used by most of the employees, and I had contributed a small four-cup mini coffee maker for decaf, for use by me and anyone else who wanted to or needed to avoid caffeine. Primarily, it was for me, though we occasionally had staff members who were pregnant or nursing or just wanted to limit caffeine intake for health concerns. Most days, I made a pathetic two cups and drank them on my own.

I haven't had caffeine in my system for 22 years, and still maintain that I can become hyper, frenzied and stressed with the best of 'em, without the help of a stimulant, thank you. Actually, I have a rapid heart rate, a condition aggravated by caffeine, and haven't noticed a difference in the taste of drinks without caffeine, especially since I don't like syrupy sweet sodas and drink coffee only a few times each week. Rarely, but on occasion I treat myself to a vanilla latte, but definitely for the taste rather than the buzz.

It was a Wednesday morning, which meant staff meetings with two of my male staff members for two hours. No one was scheduled to be there for 15 minutes, so I decided to brew a short cup of coffee. Within a few minutes, my younger daughter, April, who also worked part-time for the organization, showed up and began chatting about the day's events. With my back toward her at the kitchen counter, I reached for the coffee maker to pour in the water. I heard April's voice, but it was a distant muffled sound compared to the quiver in my chest. The second series of skipped heartbeats literally took my breath away. I realized instantly that I was losing consciousness, but I could not focus long enough to capture April's attention or call for help.

I learned later from my daughter that she had been in the

middle of telling a story about one of her college classes when she noticed I had lowered and bowed my head to the kitchen counter. At first she thought I was just being silly or playing a joke, but she heard me moan as if in pain. She saw me grasp the countertop with both hands as if to steady myself, but I didn't say a word.

Now aware of the seriousness of the situation, and with no phone available nearby, April ran to the reception desk and told the staff member to dial 911. April had just started talking to the dispatcher when she suddenly heard a series of crashes from the lunch room and realized I had collapsed. Handing the phone to the receptionist, she returned to the kitchen to find me lying on the floor. Other employees had heard the sound and came looking for the source of the commotion. They likely expected to see a lunch bag, tray of goodies or cup of coffee dropped by a clumsy, sleepy staff member. At any rate, I doubt anyone was prepared for what they actually saw.

April noticed my eyes were open, but the left eye was already beginning to swell and turn black. She put her mouth on mine and breathed twice, deeply and hopefully, into my lungs, but to no avail; she could see no response or sign of life. My eyes closed and my face turned gray. Time seemed to stand still, and for me, I suppose it did. April didn't know where to turn for help when so many people appeared to be as helpless as she felt. No one could move, as if frozen.

One of the staff I was to meet with had arrived earlier than scheduled so he could leave for an early lunch celebration with his grandson. Hearing the activity, he rushed into the lunch room and took over performing CPR and began breathing for me. As Steve worked on me chest compressions, followed by mouth-to-mouth resuscitation everyone in the room held their breath as if to offer it to me.

Suddenly, Steve's breath became mine as my chest filled and released. After several breaths, I took a long, deep gasp of air, trying to hold onto the precious gift inside my lungs. Slowly regaining consciousness, I recognized a hazy male presence. I didn't know where I was or what was happening to me, but I could hear him as he repeated, "Stay with me. Come on, Deb. Stay with me. Just breathe. Come on, you can do it. Breathe." He continued that way, his pleas ringing in my ears until they became impossible to ignore. He wasn't taking "no" for an answer, and I was believing him. As his pleas became almost military and demanding, I grew determined not to disappoint this person. I drew breaths on my own as my lungs and heart took over and began generating oxygen and blood to my exhausted and dying body.

It was as if a newborn baby was taking its first breath, struggling with the arrival of the newness of life. But, unlike a newborn, I had tasted life and knew that even with its combination of good, bad and ugly, I cherished it, and desperately wanted to hold onto it.

I began to realize that I had been given a rare gift of dual experiences. Not only did I have the advantage of sampling life, with its sweet and sour pallet, but I also now had experienced a taste of death.

I will take refuge in the shadow of your wings
until the disaster has passed. Psalm 57:1

My mind and body were awakening, and my eyes, having lost depth perception, squinted and struggled to bring the foreground into view, as my bewildered consciousness tried to rally, first by simply identifying people and things around me. As I tried to focus on Steve, my rescuer and teammate, I saw he had a look of intensity that I had never seen in him before. As an ex-cop, he usually had an air of confidence and self-control. Unlike some of the other male staff, who always wore suits and dress shirts, Steve wore jeans, a leather or jean jacket and parked his motorcycle under the portico every morning. He was a no-nonsense kind of guy, and had the respect of everyone who worked with him. He cared deeply about the young people he helped and was unashamedly a Christian, which I admired and appreciated. I knew if he looked concerned, it must be for a good reason.

I vaguely remembered where I was, that Steve had arrived at work for the meeting, and that he must have been called to help in an emergency situation. He knelt beside me, and April took my hand. I became increasingly aware of my body: my chest ached when I tried to take a slow, deep breath. It felt as if an elephant had tackled me and then wrestled me to the ground while standing on my left ankle. A dull ache generated from the left side of my head, but I didn't know why. I couldn't understand how or when I had ended up on the hard kitchen floor.

As more of the room came into blurry focus I became aware of a crowd of people standing over me with ashen faces. They looked so worried that I felt guilty for not helping them, or at least asking if they needed to sit down. Honestly, they were making me nervous.

Most were fellow employees who had gathered out of concern and curiosity, but soon I started to take note of the others who made me even more anxious. These were not friends, family or co-workers. I didn't know these people, and I tried to understand why they were there. They wore crisp, official uniforms and I recognized them as medical personnel or paramedics who evidently had arrived at the scene earlier, before I was aware of their presence. Since I was the only person lying on the floor, I assumed they were there for me, and I knew this was not a good sign.

"Oh God, let this be a horrible dream, and more importantly, let me wake up – alive."

I felt as if I were experiencing a bad dream in which I thought everyone was staring at me but didn't know why. I was unsure about the reality of the incident; was it real or a delusion? My eyes darted from face to face, trying to read their motives and intentions. I was beginning to doubt my ability to reason or discern. I thought I must be dreaming. "Oh God, let this be a horrible dream, and more importantly, let me wake up – alive."

I've heard experts and analysts say that the most common dreams we experience are about being chased, falling from a cliff and being embarrassed or naked in crowds. I quickly felt my side to happily learn that my clothing and underwear were intact, but I was still hoping to hear the morning snooze alarm. This being a dream would make life much easier, as well as provide some lively lunchtime humor. I imagined hearing the girls gathered around the conference room table commenting on their craziest dreams, like one in which a girl shows up at the reception desk in a bikini and a fur coat, or a most memorable nightmare in which squirrels run rampant in the offices. Then I would top them all with my tale: "You'll never believe this. I dreamed that I had passed out cold on the kitchen floor and everybody just kept looking at me. Then Steve started pounding on my chest to give me CPR and..."

But this was no dream and it became all too clear within a few minutes as the EMTs started asking questions about prescription medications, allergies and medical conditions. Listening to the background voices, I heard my daughter April's voice quickly answering questions on my behalf as the medics secured me to a gurney.

The flurry of activity was all too familiar for April, who I learned later was painfully recalling an incident of 12 years before that had left me unconscious and had left her, along with her sister, petrified.

April and Abby were at home with me; April was 10 at the time, and Abby was 14. Without warning, during the simple task of cleaning off the kitchen table following lunch, I experienced a sudden series of irregular heartbeats that caused me to lose consciousness. Abby thought quickly, called 911, and was told to administer CPR. As a petite girl, she wasn't able to apply the chest compressions, but by the grace of God was able to keep me alive long enough for paramedics to arrive and administer further CPR and oxygen.

The incident was traumatic for both young girls, who witnessed their mother lying on the floor, turning gray from a lack of oxygen and absence of a pulse. April felt bad for not helping Abby. Apparently she had heard the commotion from the fall and had run to the hallway from the bathroom where she had been bathing, but immediately ran back to the bedroom area, scared and confused.

After the paramedics arrived at our house and I was stabilized, they transported me to the nearest hospital in St. Louis, a city where we had lived with our family for 15 years. My parents, who lived three hours away, were contacted about the accident and were asked to help with the girls. They arrived as quickly as possible and helped call other family members. Rick had to be notified at his office where he had just started working, 1,200 miles away from home. We had recently sold our home in a suburb south of St. Louis and were waiting to pack the U-Haul to move to Orlando, Florida, where Rick had begun his new job a month earlier. Our original plan was to move together, but our real estate sales contract fell through, leaving me to stay and sell the house. It was a stressful time for our family, but we believed that God was calling us to make the move, so the setbacks didn't stop us from going forward. At the time, I felt the cardiac arrest could be attributed to flu-like symptoms along with a combination of stress and fatigue.

Now, 12 years later, in the kitchen of my workplace, April was telling the paramedics about that all-too-similar event. I tuned into the year of that incident as she spoke, and immediately corrected the date to June 1997. She and others commented on my ability to hear, comprehend, and relate the memory as a positive sign. The EMTs strapped me to the stretcher as they made a plan to take me down to the entry level of the building. Unfortunately, the elevator would not accommodate the stretcher, so the plan involved bringing me down the stairwell.

We sometimes confuse gravity with safety.

I was very aware of my surroundings as they brought me down the stairs, and I could only hope the narrow stairwell would accommodate the paramedics and me. Suddenly the metal side door of the office building flew open, letting in the morning sun, peeking through a canopy of fall leaves. The cool light air was a stark contrast to that of the dim, compact kitchen floor where I had been lying for some time.

My horizontal perspective created a sense of depth as I suddenly watched the world from a different angle. My perceptions were keenly acute, especially as I tried to take in my surroundings as we moved toward the waiting ambulance. I had walked upright on that path from my car to the office countless times, but I had never been aware of the boldness and brilliance of the sky. I wonder if our vertical position not only keeps us from looking up but also gives us a false feeling of security. We sometimes confuse gravity with safety. Actually, I'm sure most of us would be astonished at how different our surroundings would appear from a horizontal view.

I suddenly looked up to see a series of familiar faces: my frightened, concerned husband standing beside my daughter with her tear-stained, worried face and a long line of distraught friends and co-workers. My family clasped my hands briefly as the

> *As I quickly learned, this day and this perspective would change the way I looked at life – forever.*

paramedics quickly transferred me into the blue and white ambulance. Then I left them behind in the long desperate cry of the siren.

As I quickly learned, this day and this perspective would change the way I looked at life – *forever*.

Re•vive
1. To bring back to life or consciousness; resuscitate.
2. To impart new health, vigor, or spirit to.
3. To restore to use, currency, activity, or notice.
4. To restore the validity or effectiveness of.
5. To renew in the mind; recall.

(www.thefreedictionary.com)

A Long Way From Home

I am the Lord, the God of all mankind.
Is anything too hard for me? Jeremiah 32:27

The quick ambulance ride to the hospital took less than five minutes. I knew the hospital was within walking distance because I had taken the path many times. I pictured the walks I had taken on several occasions when I exchanged my lunch hour for a healthy brisk amble around the nearby park of the medical complex. I could look out my private office window to view the walking path beyond the buildings that I used for stress relief. A peaceful, serene setting lay just a few yards away. The serenity of the pond and fountain surrounded by Canada geese and mallards seemed to counter the relentless drive of the exercise enthusiasts trying to keep pace with their workout strategies.

Still, I had to admit that I sometimes envied the young mothers who took leisurely strolls with nowhere in particular to go. Some sat near the lake and picnicked with family, while others like me, from neighboring businesses, on a schedule even during their breaks, remained on a mission to accomplish a task.

On those occasions when I took walks around the park, I think I was mostly amused and a little annoyed as I passed by the congregation of hospital workers, dressed in scrubs, proudly displaying their name badges, who huddled over the nearest picnic table to inhale and release clouds of cigarette smoke. They rarely conversed, because they too were on a mission to smoke as many cigarettes as possible within their break time.

That day, as we drove up to the emergency room entrance, the thought of healthcare workers not taking their health or mine seriously was suddenly neither amusing or comforting.

The sirens were silenced as the medical team wheeled me from the ambulance to the hospital. A detailed query began as soon as I arrived at the Emergency Room, as a barrage of nurses moved quickly and skillfully to evaluate the seriousness of the situation by inundating me with questions, even as they consulted with other professionals. "Can you tell me your name? Do you know what day it is? Can you tell me the month? Did you feel faint before you passed out? Have you had anything to eat today? Are you taking any medications regularly?" As the questions were flying, my heart rate and blood pressure were monitored and an IV was started in both my arms.

Rick and April had arrived at the hospital before the ambulance, so they were waiting in the corridor to see me. The nurse's assistants immediately began removing my clothing – my tan dress slacks, dark brown fitted sweater, matching shoes and olive green business jacket. Just a couple of hours earlier I had taken great pains to bathe, choose an outfit for work and meticulously dress myself. Now, I was being disrobed by people I didn't know and who didn't know me, and being clothed in a one-size-fits-all faded blue hospital gown.

Just a few hours earlier I would never have dreamed that my morning would begin and end in such mayhem.

Just a few hours earlier I would never have dreamed that my morning would begin and end in such mayhem. The pleasant but hurried nurse's aide unhooked the necklace Rick had given me four days earlier for our anniversary. As he stood beside me in the flurry of activity, he watched helplessly as his wife was being transformed from the healthy, active, vibrant woman he had seen just hours earlier into a person who was in grave danger of losing her life and devastating his.

Upon seeing Rick, the assistant removing my silver hoop earrings stopped, quickly handed him the necklace, and raised my left hand, motioning for him to take off my wedding ring. He hesitated, but she insisted, holding my hand to steady it. As my groom, 28 years ago, he had slipped that slim band of gold and petite marquis-cut diamonds onto my hand in a private, simple ceremony with our immediate families. I'm certain in the 28 years we had been together he had never removed my rings.

Anyone familiar with my husband knows he is a very serious, sentimental man and is committed to our relationship. To someone who has a lighter personality, this moment might not have been so distressingly symbolic, but for Rick, it was devastating. Slowly, he slipped the wedding set down my thin finger and cradled it in his hand for a moment. He could feel the warmth from my body, and the scent from the hand cream I had applied that morning left a fragrant residue. The nurse gave him the clear plastic bag containing the other jewelry, and the medical team wheeled me out toward the entrance doors to perform a CT scan on my skull.

Suddenly, I found myself in an enclosed cylinder as technicians gave deliberate and distinct instructions, alternating between "hold your breath" and "now breathe." From the moment I regained consciousness I had continued to complain that the pain in my left ankle and foot was unbearable. My chest ached from Steve's CPR compressions. I was sure something must be broken. My skull continued to ache dully on the left and top, but I was unclear about the fall and injury.

Slowly, he slipped the wedding set down my thin finger and cradled it in his hand for a moment.

The scan wasn't uncomfortable, but shortly after the procedure began, an excruciating pain shot through my head, like a knife being forced into my skull. I had never experienced this kind of agony. I didn't know what was happening to me as my head pulsed relentlessly. Pulling the oxygen tube from my nose and clutching my head, I cried out for relief. I wanted to reach into my head and pull out my skull. As I tore at the neck brace and anything else I could reach, the doctors and nurses realized something was terribly wrong. I had not had this kind of reaction to pain earlier.

Our pastor arrived at the hospital shortly after April's mass text. Several others from the organization where I worked and church friends arrived later and began praying and helping April and Rick to focus on God and His provisions rather than the constant ticking of the clock.

The neurosurgeon's physician's assistant approached my husband and told him there was an immediate need for surgery. The scan had shown an arterial bleed and hematoma that were causing the pain between the skull and the membrane surrounding the brain. The urgent need to stop the swelling and bleeding had reached a critical moment. The surgeon explained that if he did not operate immediately, there would not be sufficient time to halt the bleeding and save my life. The left side of my brain was hemorrhaging and precious seconds counted. The surgeon quickly explained the delicate surgery procedure to my husband and daughter, "We have got to go in and stop the bleeding from her brain. We will shave her head, cut out a portion of her skull and hopefully stop the bleeding."

Rick related that he remembered me having said earlier, "Please don't let them operate on me." He hesitated as my words lingered but April looked at her dad and said, "We don't have a choice. We have to do this." Knowing it was true, he nodded his head in approval and told the surgeons to proceed with the surgery.

The hospital bed engulfed my tiny, lifeless body as tubes and equipment hemmed me in on all sides. Rick probed the sheets for my right hand as April searched for the left. Not knowing how she would handle her initial reaction and emotions, April remembered that Lane, our pastor, had coached her to read scripture to me because my spirit could respond to the truths even if my mind and body could not. Her initial response had been, "I don't want to upset Mom and make her think she is dying." As she read the words, she realized they were as much for her comfort as mine.

The nurses continued to prepare me for surgery. Within seconds they whisked me down the corridor and into the operating room, where they would work feverishly for four hours. At one point in the procedure, the surgeon later related, when he opened my skull to repair the damage and bleeding, a portion of the skull fell out onto the operating table. Within approximately two hours after the surgery began, the hematoma measured three to five times larger than when it had first been detected on the original CT scan. The neurosurgeon told Rick and April that it was fortunate that they had been able to operate as quickly as they did because timing was a significant factor.

With the surgery complete, the next stage in the process

consisted of observation and waiting. Only more time would tell whether my speech would be affected and interrupted or if more extensive surgery was necessary, in the event that the bleeding inside my head continued. It was amazing that the initial problem had been caused by cardiac arrest, but that the brain injury from the subsequent fall had now become the crisis that superseded everything.

Waiting and Praying

Our older daughter Abby drove from St. Louis and arrived after the surgery and was made aware of the possible repercussions from the surgery. Other out-of-town family members were called, as well as friends who were notified about the incident and surgery and were asked to pray. Mass texts and emails were sent literally around the world as the news spread. Prayer groups and individuals spent hours lifting up their hearts for their sister in Christ who needed a touch from the "great physician." I know the sounds of God's people praying on behalf of a fellow believer were a sweet music savored by a Holy Savior eager to answer their prayers. I was quickly reminded that Daniel 9:23 in the old testament of the Bible says, *"As soon as you began to pray, an answer was given...."*

And while I lay sleeping, my family, friends and even

...often in life, a moment changes the message forever.

Christians who did not know me personally prayed, knocking upon and even storming the door of heaven on my behalf. To know this is happening is an awesome realization, especially when you are on the receiving end.

I urge you never to take those emails, messages or texts lightly when you are asked to take a moment and pray for someone. Doing so makes a radical difference in the lives of those in need, and in the life of the one who prays.

Listen to my cry for help, my King and my God, for to you I pray.   Psalm 5:2

When Abby arrived at the hospital, she was visibly shaken. I had sent the initial "happy birthday" voice mail that morning but she had accidentally deleted it after hearing the words and message. The very next message was from her frantic sister saying I had collapsed from cardiac arrest and was being rushed to the local hospital. Her eyes stung with tears as she clutched the phone with regret, wishing she would have saved the original words. She suddenly longed to hear her mother's voice again, but often in life, a moment changes the message forever.

Immediately after hearing the news, she drove as quickly as possible from St. Louis, where she had been working and living for the past two weeks. Her thoughts rewound to the scene of a young 14 year old, 12 years earlier, when she had been the one to try to give the kiss of life to her mother. She had been terrified, unprepared as she was for anything so frightening or life-altering. Blinking her eyes and shaking her head, she now tried to rid herself of the lingering thoughts that she had worked so hard to forget, but the memories persisted as she raced to the hospital, fearing the worst but hoping for the best.

The surgery finished, I rested in the neuro-intensive care unit, still under the affects of anesthesia. Rick, Abby and April took turns holding my hand as the medical staff constantly monitored my condition at my bedside.

As April took my limp hand, I focused on her familiar face. With a soft, weak voice, I drew her closer and asked two questions, "Did they cut my hair?" With the corner of one side of her mouth rising, she nodded affirming my concern. And then, I started to whimper like a small child and responded, "Did they at least leave some bangs?" Fighting inappropriate laughter mixed with sorrow and compassion, she managed a smile accompanied by tears as she realized that her mother had been temporarily protected from the reality of her critical condition.

Throughout the evening watch, nurses took vital signs, drew blood, administered steroids and assessed my coherence along with any ability to communicate. By now, the left eye and cheek were swollen to a deep purple, leaving me unable to focus or see any distance.

Often, the room was dim but a nurse would suddenly

appear with a flashlight to shine in my face in the night to ask me my name, the date, who the president was, and where I was (hospital, town and state). The verbal drill included pushing and pulling my feet against the force of the nurse's hands, touching the nurse's finger in front of her without moving my head, while alternating touching my nose and then her finger. Several times during the day and night shifts, that test was followed by a request to do a series of facial expressions: puff out your cheeks, stick out your tongue and move it to the left and right of your mouth, smile showing your teeth, and bug out your eyes. Bugging out my eyes was not a problem, because the obnoxious flashlight always caused an involuntary response from my exhausted pupils.

Eventually, I was asked to alternate raising my left and right leg off the bed. All of these exercises would happen within seconds of the flashlight interrogations, which the nurses executed with all the delicacy of a drill sergeant in a rookie platoon unit. With one eye closed from the swelling and having had head surgery, followed by pain killers and morphine, I would say that I probably did not score well. But I kept getting the same test again and again for the entire hospital stay.

Like Pavlov's dog, I soon became conditioned to and familiar with the drill, and began to immediately stick out my tongue and puff my cheeks when a nurse came into my room. I began to wonder if these exercises were to test your neurological and mental ability or your sheer desire to preserve your own sanity. I'm not sure I would score very high on any given day, hospitalized or not, especially upon being awakened in the middle of the night.

The first and second evenings at the hospital were the most challenging. I'm sure the nurses had been trained precisely what to look for in these testing procedures to evaluate head trauma victims. Most were kind and even apologized for interrupting my sleep and rest.

...many of us... hoped... that the death angel wasn't... calling one of our names.

However, on one of the first nights after I had regained consciousness, one of the nurses on duty came into my room without an apology or a smile. Like Santa without the jolly disposition, she spoke not a word but went straight to her work. She pulled back the curtains that helped close off the ICU room from the light and bustle of the front desk. The row of intensive care rooms flanked the nurses' station, where patients were monitored 24 hours a day to make certain that a nurse was aware of all vital signs and was on hand to address any emergencies that might arise.

More than once, especially at night, I remember hearing the eerie sound of an otherwise pleasant but monotone female voice on the hospital corridor intercom repeating the calm appeal, "Code blue, code blue, code blue stat." The voice would often announce the floor number, but I wondered how many of us in the ICU hoped the plea for help would not bring a flurry of health care professionals prepared to test their life-saving skills and dedication to the Hippocratic oath – and more realistically, that the death angel wasn't ringing our bell or calling one of our names.

After opening the curtains, the nurse returned to my bedside to continue her inquiry into my ability to express emotions and communicate. If I had been in a more normal state of mind, and been able to fully speak my mind, it probably would not have been my kindest hour. Beaming the flashlight into my face, the nurse quickly began to check cognitive skills, facial movements and expressions. Aside from squinting and grimacing, my confused brain and tired body weren't able to respond immediately. For each instruction, after a few moments, I tried my best to perform the tasks she wanted from me.

Then, I remembered that I had the bed sheet, crumpled and clinched in my left fist, holding on tightly to a piece of what I perceived as a memory breakthrough. Excitedly, I proceeded to try to tell the nurse about the field of miniature ponies I had visited where the horses were beautifully groomed with pastel-colored ribbons in their manes. I went on as if to build on the evidence. My granddaughter was at the farm, too, with some other neighborhood children who came to enjoy the circus. The big-top tents were made of sheets woven together.

I called to my husband to defend me to the nurse, who seemed annoyed rather than enlightened by the story. He walked closer to the bed, but I saw his hesitancy. Then the nurse shook her head in frustration and disbelief, motioning to my husband, who was now standing beside me. I made eye contact with him for some reassurance, but he avoided my gaze, and had a look of pity and compassion for me.

I became anxious for someone – anyone – to believe me, and to give me a chance to prove that I wasn't crazy. Remembering the bed sheet I held tightly in my hand, I pulled it toward my face to prove my case. "Look, this sheet was at the farm where the ponies were. You've got to believe me."

I became anxious for someone – anyone – to believe me, and to give me a chance to prove that I wasn't crazy.

The nurse said to my husband, as if I were invisible, "This is something new. She hasn't done this before." I was very aware of her body language and tone of voice that said, "Things aren't right, she isn't making sense, something is terribly wrong." Rick tried reasoning with me, but the more he tried to console me, the more defensive and agitated I became. I remember feeling that everyone was against me and fearing that I would be considered insane. I thought of a movie I had seen where a lady whose son was missing was trying to tell authorities that he had been kidnapped or stolen, but no one believed her, and eventually the authorities put her in an insane asylum. I feared from the nurse's reaction, as well as my husband's, that I was on the verge of being institutionalized. Looking back, I have to remember that I had been given morphine following the brain surgery and that had an affect on my thinking, not to mention the swelling in the brain and extended trauma.

My thoughts during that first evening, which was actually the same day as the surgery, were disturbing for me also. I had the idea that the surgeons had cut my hair, but that each section of hair had been given to a person or couple, and each piece of hair had become an embryo. I was crying, upset that I had given away all the hair, six sections to be exact, but that my older daughter, Abby, who didn't have children and wanted that opportunity, had been left out. And I couldn't help her, and this was my only chance. I remember that one of the hair/embryo recipients was Kate, from the reality show "Jon and Kate Plus 8," and I remember thinking, *She doesn't need any more kids, so how did she end up with my embryo hair?*

> *I couldn't control my emotions, and it took some time to convince myself that what I was thinking was not real.*

I couldn't control my emotions, and it took some time to convince myself that what I was thinking was not real. I kept playing the scenario over and over in my head trying to separate the truth from the imaginary. I couldn't seem to distinguish dreams and visions or hallucinations from truth, even though people were trying to help me.

It's amazing how delicate God designed our brains and thoughts to be. I began not to trust the nurses or others in my room, but I also began to realize that I couldn't trust myself either. I would drift off to sleep but not remember time lapses, where I was, or who I might have talked to just minutes earlier. I reasoned about things, and challenged myself to be sure that what I was thinking was real and truthful. I quickly became very aware of the truth of 2 Corinthians 10:5, which states, *"...and we take captive every thought to make it obedient to Christ."* I knew that I had to have the mind of Christ, literally, to have any understanding of what was happening. I determined that until I could speak more clearly and coherently, before I spoke I would review in my mind how whatever I had to say might sound to others.

Lying quietly throughout the night, I was concerned that I might fall asleep and experience more elaborate dreams and visions. As I said, I was paranoid enough to fear being labeled as unstable, or even insane, or to be thought of as having brain damage. I made it a goal to rehearse any thought I might have in my mind before verbalizing and sharing it. Initially, I realized that my speech needed to be clearer and my memory sharper for me to be able to form intelligible words.

All night I practiced reciting the alphabet to myself. I found it hard to believe that something so elementary could be so hard to remember. I began strong with the first six letters, until I came to "g." Starting over and over, I finally came to the end of the alphabet by morning. My mind and body were exhausted. I was told later by the nurse that my brain needed rest more than exercise to allow it to heal. Now they told me!

An Unexpected Gift

... "No eye has seen, no ear has heard, no mind has conceived what God has prepared for those who love him."   1 Corinthians 2:9

Great peace have they who love your law, and nothing can make them stumble. Psalm 119:165

I awoke to the sound of paper rustling in the background. Not knowing who it might be, I listened for the voice of a nurse. Instead, I sensed the presence of someone familiar as I heard a female voice quietly clear her throat and leaf through the pages of a book. She sat in an armchair out of my view, but I recognized the silhouette as that of my daughter, April. She apparently had been reading to me when I drifted off to sleep. When I woke up, my short-term memory, adversely affected by the head trauma and subsequent surgery, had robbed me of any remembrance of a previous conversation.

April had determined to sit by my bedside and read scripture to me, hoping and praying for God's intervention for a breakthrough healing. Moments like these were not encouraging, especially when I couldn't remember her being with me or reading anything.

I didn't have a good memory, but I had heard doctors and nurses talking in a concerned tone.

Keeping her promise to herself and others, April continued her vigil, partly to give her father a break, and partly because she considered the time with me a blessing for both of us. When she heard me shifting in the bed, she pulled her chair closer.

She asked if I needed anything and then if I wanted her to read some more. I told her I appreciated her being with me and that I wanted to tell her something I hadn't shared with anyone else. I wasn't alert, but I knew my condition was serious. I didn't have a good memory, but I had heard doctors and nurses talking in a concerned tone. I was being attended around the clock, and volumes of fluids and tubes were being fed into and out of my body from various angles.

I kept my eyes closed as I slowly said to April, "I was afraid." I paused as tears began to stream down my cheeks. My voice cracked as I struggled to form the words. "I was afraid that I wasn't going to make it." I took a deep breath in and out of my sore chest and finished the thought, "I thought that I would die." I heard her shift in her seat as I continued to weep. She didn't say a word, but I heard her sniff and then take a tissue from the hospital tray. I continued, "But I'm beginning to think that I'm going to be alright."

She quickly spoke to support my positive attitude, chiming in, "Yes, you are going to be fine – I just know it – God is going to help you."

Knowing April was listening intently, I felt that I wanted someone to know my wishes in case I did not survive. This was a difficult thing for me to do because I had never discussed death with any of my family. We had had deaths in our family, of course, but most were of elderly family members, and were the result of age-related illnesses that came as no surprise. No one ever hinted at the possibility of someone not recovering from an illness, as if doing so was a bad omen or negative confession – as if talking about the possibility of death would curse the sick person.

I explained why I continued to keep the dress after almost 30 years.

At the risk of a curse, I proceeded to tell April that even though I felt I would recover, I wanted her to know that I would have wanted certain things for my funeral. I asked her if she remembered seeing a deep purple silk dress with white wispy leaves hanging in my closet. She didn't respond, but I explained why I continued to keep the dress after almost 30 years. It was the first article of clothing her father had ever purchased and given me.

We had met for lunch to celebrate Valentine's Day and afterwards went to the Jewel Box in St. Louis's Forest Park. Upon our arrival at the Botanical Garden, he presented me with a beautifully wrapped package containing a dress that I had tried on and modeled for him in a local department store earlier that week. He had paid attention to details in so many ways, and I not only loved the dress, but was touched by his thoughtfulness. I hadn't worn the dress for many years, but I wanted to keep it with me always.

While I lay in my hospital bed, songs ran through my mind, and there were two particular melodies that had given me peace and wonderful memories as a child and later as an adult. I often referred to the movie, "The Wizard of Oz," as a favorite of mine. It was aired once each year on the one television station we received. As a child, I memorized the words and would stand on our picnic table in the backyard singing "Somewhere Over the Rainbow" at the top of my lungs.

As an adult, I first heard "It is Well with My Soul" while attending Bible Study Fellowship, a weekly, in-depth international study in which the books of the bible are covered over a six-year period of time. It was a simple church setting with a piano accompaniment featuring more than 400 women harmoniously singing,

> When peace like a river attendeth my way,
> When sorrows like sea billows roll.
> Whatever my lot, Thou hast taught me to say,
> "It is well, it is well with my soul."

I paused to think about the words and the writer who composed them out of personal tragedy and spiritual triumph. For many years, I could not have honestly voiced those words. Now, lying in what could have been my death-bed, there was apprehension and fear, but also an overriding peace that assured me no matter the outcome, it was "well with my soul."

> *For I am convinced that neither death nor life, neither angels nor demons, neither the present nor the future, nor any powers, neither height nor depth, nor anything else in all creation, will be able to separate us from the love of God that is in Christ Jesus our Lord.* Romans 8:38-39

While I don't like to discuss death, I know the Bible tells us in Hebrews 9:27 that *"... it is appointed for man to die once, and after that comes judgment."* (ESV) Based on my salvation experience, I was confident in my relationship with God. But there is something about coming to the threshold of death and eternity that can make you want to hold on to this life. Of course, that isn't true for everyone, and I believe God can give people the grace to step into heaven with no fear or dread. It will be a wonderful experience.

Corrie ten Boom once told a story about God's grace and ability to equip us for anything He has planned for us, including death. She simply explained that we often don't understand something because it is not for us or "our time." She explained that when a person is going on a journey, it is the one getting on the train who needs a ticket. Everyone at the train station doesn't get or need a ticket, only the passengers. When it is time to get on the train, the passenger will know, get their ticket, and gladly board the train. It evidently wasn't time for me to get on the train. I wanted to live and to stay with my family, and felt that there was something I still needed to do.

...I blinked my heavy eyelids, sensing someone standing over me.

That night, I blinked my heavy eyelids, sensing someone standing over me. There were so many nurses coming in and out of the room that I rarely acknowledged or noticed them. But, even through the effects of the drugs and trauma, I recognized the dimly lit silhouette as that of our daughter, Abby. Her eyes were teary as she approached the hospital bed, and her face was stained with make-up that had begun to smear. Smiling, she bent over the metal bed rail to kiss my forehead. "I brought you something," she said.

Pulling something made of silk in muted colors from behind her back, she placed it next to me. I realized it was a doll, a stuffed Precious Moments doll with praying hands. When Abby was a child, she loved playing with most dolls, whether Cabbage Patch, Barbie, Babysitter or American Girl. They were all special to her, and she spent hours playing with them along with her younger sister, as they pretended to be mothers and teachers.

The gift spoke volumes, because Abby's love language is gifts. If she wants you to know that she cares for you, she is a very thoughtful giver. When she was a young teen, she saved her allowance and earnings from babysitting to buy me an expensive, ornate, hand-painted teapot. It was beautiful, and I knew she had sacrificed to buy something of value because that was how she felt about me. A couple years later, she saved nearly $300 of her hard-earned money while working at a local YMCA after-school program to buy a special piece of framed artwork by Thomas Kinkade, the well-known artist. We had browsed in mall stores months prior to her purchase when she had heard me admiring the painting. For Abby, her love and appreciation are expressed in gift-giving.

Abby felt helpless as she stood near me, but wanted to say that she cared.

This day was no different. Abby felt helpless as she stood near me, but wanted to say that she cared. I thanked her for her thoughtfulness as relief flooded my spirit. Lately, I hadn't known or felt that she wanted to be anywhere near me. Abby stayed for a while, holding and stroking my hand, avoiding the IVs and monitors. She has a needle phobia and has literally fainted from the mere sight or mention of them. Finally, excusing herself from the room, she bent over my bed to tell me that she would be back later. As she did, her hand inadvertently pressed the doll's tummy, causing a recording to begin. The words were familiar as the large-eyed doll began, "Now I lay me down to sleep…" Abby looked surprised that the voice was coming from the doll, and apparently didn't realize it had come with a recorded prayer. At the moment the words began, "if I should die before I wake…," my emotions were triggered, not because of the prayer, but at how important it was that Abby was with me and cared enough to bring a gift with a sentimental meaning. She needed to go; it had been a moment of unspoken feelings and understanding. I felt more loved by her than I had in quite some time. My heart felt lighter and more peaceful knowing that burden was lifted.

Later, I listened to the recording again, remembering the times I had recited that prayer with my children at bedtime. We replaced the line that said, "If I should die before I wake, I pray the Lord my soul to take," to make the prayer more kid-friendly: "I pray You take me through the night and wake me with Your morning light." The soft silk doll lay beside me all that night, and when I woke the following day, I smiled, grateful for answered prayer.

Both daughters, Abby and April, spent time each day and night with me, as did my husband, who stayed by my side with only short breaks to go to the bathroom or grab a bite from the cafeteria. Many meals were brought to and eaten in my room. Even in the night or when I was in a groggy, weakened state, I could detect my family's individual scents and movements. I knew their touch when I would wake up to find them caressing my hand or whispering a prayer in the still of the night. Each one had his or her own unique approach to being close to me and expressing love.

April has a gift for inspiring others and brightening any day or circumstance. She will be an elementary teacher upon graduation and although she is intelligent, her biggest asset is her ability to bring relationship and add life to the mundane. Working part-time, attending classes and caring for her three-year-old daughter, she still came to the hospital to be with me every day. The mood and setting in the room was mostly solemn, dim, and quiet apart from the clinical and medical procedures.

...none of us really takes the time to appreciate these moments, unless they are threatened, or worse, if we have missed the opportunity and are left with regrets.

She smiled each time she came, kissing my forehead and sitting next to my bed while reading books to me, much as I had done for her as a child.

She and the others had a tremendous impact on my will to fight to regain strength and energy. I'm sure I would have never known their special closeness in this way otherwise, because none of us really takes the time to appreciate these moments, unless they are threatened, or worse, if we have missed the opportunity and are left with regrets.

My mother used to say that she always appreciated when people gave her flowers, because she felt people should give them while you're alive, rather than waiting to send large bouquets to the funeral home or gravesite. "Give flowers to the living," she would say. Many times, our home would have a vase of fresh-cut roses, begonias or wild flowers from our garden sitting on the kitchen table with the aroma wafting throughout the farmhouse. As a child I would gather black-eyed Susans or Easter lilies to surprise and delight my mom. She would always respond with a surprised grin. My mind drifted to my mother and how I would love to see her and spend time with her. Unfortunately, she was diagnosed with early onset Alzheimer's disease in her early sixties and over the past few years, her mental abilities had declined quickly. She could no longer speak or care for herself as she moved into the latter stages of the fatal disease.

... I immediately thought of my mother and remembered her smile and her appreciation for the simplicity of life.

My thoughts drifted in and out of sleep when suddenly the double glass sliding door that opened to the NICU nurses' station exposed my room to what appeared to be thousands of high wattage light bulbs. Walking into my room, the nurse came over to my husband to tell him that another plant had been delivered for me and they would put it with the others.

It was hard to see the desk because of the lights and my limited eyesight, but Rick pointed to the nurses' counter, lined with a variety of mums, miniature roses, orange tulips, and several beautiful lush green house plants. Smiling, I immediately thought of my mother and remembered her smile and her appreciation for the simplicity of life. I'm sure I had never appreciated flowers and plants as much as at that moment. I saw that each arrangement had been sent by an individual or group who cared enough about me to choose a plant and to share a thought or sentiment.

Each one was as beautiful and unique in its design and arrangement as the person who had chosen that particular gift of a plant or flower. My friend and former supervisor had brought a bright, sassy burnt orange and bright yellow pot of mums. A group of mentors from work had sent a thoughtful floral arrangement with a soft white bear and get-well mylar balloon. Several family members from out of town wired a fall basket of lush dark greenery combined with heart-shaped vines and purple cabbage, and a very sweet, soft-spoken lady from church personally brought pale yellow petite roses to my room.

More gifts followed, and each time, I took time to study their appearance and think about the one who had chosen it for me; their personalities and the relationships I had shared with them made it easy to remember each person who brought the floral gifts. I finally understood what my mother had meant when she said, "Flowers are living and beautiful, and they should be enjoyed while you're alive." I was certainly grateful to be alive, and enjoyed the flowers. I couldn't wait to get home to actually see them up close and smell their sweet fragrance. And, in the meantime, the nurses and other visitors could enjoy their beauty, too.

Face in the Mirror

*I waited patiently for the Lord; he turned
to me and heard my cry.* Psalm 40:1

The 72-hour period that followed the brain surgery was a critical time in terms of the neurosurgeons' confidence that the surgery would prove to be successful. The strategic plan was to prevent the artery from continuing to bleed in my brain and to provide consistent draining for the buildup of fluid. CT scans were done each day to help the doctors foresee any additional problems before they might arise. At one point, about halfway through the critical period, the specialists became concerned when the CT scan appeared to show additional bleeding behind the skull, a subdural hematoma bleeding into the brain cavity. This setback made for tense moments for the doctors and my family for a period of time throughout the following day. After another follow-up scan, the doctors were relieved to find that the bleeding was minimal, and they expected the slight bleeding to eventually be absorbed into the tissue. Of course, the nurses and doctors watched carefully to be sure no additional surprises appeared, but eventually the eminent danger began to ebb with each ticking of the clock.

Slowly, the days of recovery began with minimal but consistent gains in strength and improvements over the next three days. My appetite slowly returned as strawberry gelatin was introduced and rediscovered by my long-denied taste buds. My husband placed the cool, ruby colored square near my lips and I immediately welcomed the quivering fare as nourishment. Anyone watching me consume the snack would have thought it a delicacy, as I savored every taste and requested more. I could see that the nurses and my husband were delighted at my response and my ability to eat and respond.

After I had spent four days in the neuro-intensive care unit, the critical care patient beds filled up, so the doctors determined to move me to another floor, since I had passed the 72 hours and seemed to be steadily making improvement. Surgeons would remove the drain tube from my brain and then transfer me to the cardiac floor, since the episode had begun with a cardiac arrest. I prepared for the change in scenery, but I knew the nursing staff in the NICU was top notch, and I had become familiar with them and knew most by name. There is a special bond with a nurse who sees you at your weakest and neediest and gives you sponge baths, changes your gowns, cleans up accidents and shows compassion and respect. It is a very vulnerable, humbling time. None of us believe we will be at that point until we are elderly, but that isn't always the case. And even if we are older, that doesn't make the embarrassment less difficult to bear.

By early afternoon on the fifth day after I had been admitted, the two-foot-long drain tube was strategically removed from my skull. The round plastic tube had lain coiled around my head and chest since the implantation. Having the embedded cylindrical hose pulled out of the base of my skull caused me to grimace and protest the pain, causing both daughters to quickly exit the room. Relieved to have one less bodily intrusion, I welcomed the nurses entering my private room to prepare me for the cardiac patient floor change. With the hospital staff gathering and packing my things, I was suddenly sharing my hospital bed with a variety of lovely parting gifts that included a rose-colored, molded plastic ensemble of a pitcher, drinking cup, and bedpan.

When the bed returned, it would be ready for a new guest. I couldn't help but wonder what suffering the next person might have to endure, or whether he or she would be as fortunate as I was to survive. As attendants transferred me from the NICU to the cardiac bed, the two young men secured me between the sheets and lifted me to the new bed. I had a feeling that they would have loved to engage me in a simulated game of water balloon toss if I had been a good sport. I thanked them for their help and told them that I hoped they could find their way back to the previous floor. They grinned but I could tell they didn't have a clue that I was joking. The curtains were

> *The combination of obnoxious smells, piercing sounds, and blinding lights made me abnormally uncomfortable...*

pulled as we had landed in the scenic window section of the room. The eighth floor cardiac unit of the hospital provided a new variety of sounds and smells, reeking of cafeteria food and cleaning products. In addition to the unusual hospital odor, I quickly became aware that the other side of the room, separated by only a thin blue plaid curtain, was occupied by another patient. For the first time since my hospital stay I would share a small space with another person who was also ill. Until now, I hadn't even been aware of my own body, but the move heightened my awareness. I suddenly became uncomfortable with my surroundings, not having the confidence and familiarity I had come to know with the NICU staff.

I couldn't see my roommate, but realized how mobile the patients were on this floor compared to the ICU, where most of us had been confined to our beds. All of the bright lighting and the flurry of activity seemed strange to me after the more serious attention I had been given in the days prior to the transfer. My roommate was chatting on the phone to her friend as she struggled to talk over the blaring television program in the background. The combination of obnoxious smells, piercing sounds, and blinding lights made me abnormally uncomfortable with my surroundings. I wondered if the head trauma had affected me in more adverse ways than I had predicted, or at best if I had been moved to a less critical care unit too early.

My husband nervously looked at his watch, counting the minutes and then more than an hour passed without any medical personnel coming into my room to connect the heart monitor or check on their new patient. Finally, Rick made his way to the front desk to inquire about their inattentiveness. Immediately, two nurses came to my room with apologies and explanations. Apparently they were accustomed to having the staff who bring the new patient from another floor get them connected to monitors and make the floor's nurses aware of their particular needs. Immediately the heart monitor was connected so the front desk could observe my heart's rate and activity.

Finally, the lights were dimmed, but the lady in the bed next to mine left the TV turned up throughout the ten o'clock news. Since the television was positioned between the two patient beds, it was impossible for me not to see or hear it. I was exhausted from the day and the room transition. I desperately wanted to go to sleep before the next shift of nurses poked my finger, gave me a steroid shot or drew blood. Being on a different floor didn't mean that I didn't know what the normal routine should be. Suddenly, above the roar of the TV a louder sound erupted. Rick and I looked at each other with a knowing glance. We knew my roommate wasn't watching TV because she was sleeping – sleeping with a serious snoring problem, that is. Turning off the TV sound seemed like a good idea, but the incessant snoring continued all night with no possibility of drowning it out.

Several times, nurses came in to take vital signs, draw blood and give steroid injections. By now, every finger was blue and felt like my grandmother's pin cushion. It was becoming increasingly difficult to find a vein to draw blood samples, so the nurses began exploring anything that rose to the surface.

The snoring seemed to subside, but I learned that the reprieve was because it was a shift change and the sleeping was over. As soon as the nurses began making their rounds, the lady in the next bed hit the remote and started dialing her cell phone. I was too tired to care, but I heard her telling her friend that she was being released today, so her friend could come pick her up from the hospital. I sighed as I thought of having the room to myself and possibly getting some rest after she went home.

When breakfast was delivered to my bed, my husband went to get a bite to eat in the cafeteria, and I determined to appreciate my surroundings, because I saw this move as a step closer to getting better and going home. The morning nurse later asked if she could do anything for me, and I responded that I would like some help to the bathroom because I had been using a bedpan or portable potty chair in addition to the catheter. She gladly accommodated me and I made my way to the facilities without a problem.

I was very weak, and my swollen, broken ankle and foot made it difficult to stand. Given the more immediate emergency needs of my head and heart, the sprain and broken bones in my foot had been ignored even though my left foot was black and was swollen to three times its normal size. It was painful, and I was unable to put any weight on it, but to be upright and mobile for the first time in five days was an amazing accomplishment.

With my IV pole and catheter in tow, the nurse helped me first to the toilet and then to the sink to wash my hands. This was a first since I had been admitted to the hospital, so I felt good about the achievement. Slowly, I ran the cool water over my skin, establishing my balance. Bending forward toward the porcelain sink and then glancing up into the mirror, I was shocked and startled to see the image standing before me.

> *I looked again and then quickly looked away as if I had seen a grotesque creature...*

At first, I thought it was the nurse or maybe my roommate in the background or even a distorted image from the TV. I looked again and then quickly looked away as if I had seen a grotesque creature, but couldn't help but look to satisfy a morbid curiosity.

When the realization finally hit me that the reflection was actually me, I couldn't get to the hospital bed fast enough. I was holding my breath, not because I didn't want to breathe, but because I couldn't help but wonder whether this was one of those horrible visions I had experienced on the ICU floor. Maybe I was having another hallucination.

At this point, realizing I was hallucinating would have

come as a welcome relief. Surely, I couldn't look that horrible. My hair had been shaved to the scalp on only one side of my head, with my remaining original shoulder-length hair matted with shades of dark brown, gray and dried blood. The left side of my face was black and blue, with bruises circling my eye, eyelid and my entire cheek.

I knew I was going to lose consciousness... "Oh, God. Please help me."

The night before the morning of the cardiac arrest and emergency, I had gotten my hair colored, cut and styled at an upscale beauty salon in downtown Springfield. My husband had gotten me a gift certificate there, and I had made two trips before a stylist could work me in that evening after work at 6:30. Following my appointment, I had driven home at 8:30 that night, hungry and exhausted from working all day and from having driven an extra hour, but loving my new hairdo. I'm not one to spend a lot of money on my hair or anything else, so it was a real treat for me to have the opportunity to enjoy the pampering. But now, seeing only half of it in the mirror on the distorted figure where I was standing was very much like the hallucinations from the morphine that I had experienced just days before.

Immediately, the attending nurse realized that I was visibly upset but wasn't sure what was wrong. Helping me to the side of the room where the curtain was pulled and my husband was waiting, she helped me to get seated safely.

Rick suggested that maybe I would like to sit in a chair to eat my lunch when it came a little later. I agreed and sat down and began to sob. "I had no idea. I just can't believe how horrible I look," I said. Rick tried to comfort me by saying that I had been through surgery and had been through a great deal of trauma and that I was getting better. His words were of no consolation at the time, but I did my best to restrain my emotions. Suddenly, I felt my heart skip a beat and my head go limp and drop to my chest. I knew I was going to lose consciousness, but I was helpless to stop it. I just said to myself, "Oh, God. Please help me."

Touched by an Angel

I will refresh the weary and satisfy the faint. Jeremiah 31:25

The next few moments brought a sudden rush of nurses coming to my aid. I remember waking up and immediately feeling I could not control my bowels. I began to cry to the nurses on both sides, who had asked my husband to step into the hall. I became frantic to tell them what I knew was going to happen and what I wanted desperately to prevent. I felt my intestines were going to explode, and I didn't want the embarrassment or the mess and wanted to spare everyone the humiliation. But the team was focused on getting me back to bed, so they were less concerned about messes or my less-important concerns. Immediately, the head nurse noticed that the heart monitor was not connected and had not been able to record the heart arrhythmia episode.

The nurses approached the situation aggressively and in a fast-paced, feverish work mode as they tried to determine why their newest patient had collapsed shortly after arriving. In a mood of intense focus, the nurses placed me in the hospital bed. In my disorientation, I continued to cry. The head nurse came to me with a smile of compassion, but even more, there was something special in her kind, knowing eyes. Gently, she bent to put her face close to mine. Undisturbed by what she had seen, heard or experienced, she looked deep into my eyes. Then, she placed her cheek against mine and stroked my face with the palm of her hand. In a soft voice, she said, "It's alright. You'll be fine. I've been where you are and I know how you feel."

For the first time since being in the hospital, I saw this person not as a skilled nurse but as someone who had been through pain and problems and understood what I was going through. As she raised her head and smiled at me, I saw her gray spiked hair about two inches long all over her head. She was still holding my hand as she reiterated in a confident, positive tone, "Trust me. It's going to be okay." I believed her as I continued to hold tightly to her hand.

Looking at her intently, I found myself thinking about someone other than myself, and I asked, "What did you mean when you said that you've been here? What happened to you?"

She simply smiled. "It was breast cancer. I recently underwent aggressive treatment, so I really do know how you feel. I have been exactly where you are," she said. I understood just what she meant. Our diseases and physical problems weren't the same, but we shared feelings of fear, fatigue, and frailty. She then moved into her professional role as caregiver and explained that they were going to transfer me back to the NICU because they thought it would be best to monitor me more closely after the episode. Within a few minutes, she was gone and I was being transferred again from sheet to sheet to the next bed. I didn't know her name, whether she had a family, whether she was now cancer-free and in remission, or any other details about her. But God knew I needed someone who could minister not only to my weak body and delicate emotions, but to my fragile spirit. That nurse will probably never know how she helped me; she had the influence of an angel.

April arrived shortly after the frantic activity in the cardiac room only to find me being readied to be moved again. She hugged me and turned to walk back toward her dad to tell him that she was going to get a soda. After a few steps, she caught herself on the straight-backed chair against the wall. I heard her say to her dad that she didn't feel well and that she was going to faint. She was right. Within seconds, her body went limp and she began to lose her balance.

The nurses had stepped from my room momentarily so Rick couldn't leave my side until the heart monitor was in place and working. Rushing to support April and lower her to the floor, he frantically called out into the hallway for assistance from a young student nurse walking past the room. She enlisted additional help and another nurse came to the room, sitting April in a chair while giving her juice to elevate her electrolytes. After a revived April admitted that she had skipped breakfast, the sense of panic that had pervaded the room subsided, and she regained strength.

Upon arriving on the original NICU floor where I had been since my hospital admittance, I was assigned a new room. Since they all looked the same to me and my eyesight had been compromised after the accident, I would never have known the difference. Several of the nurses who had cared for me over the past week came to my bedside. Some were curious about what had prompted the move back to the ICU, and others just wanted to come by to say "hi" and help with the next stage in my care. This time, I had many of the same staff, but because of my short-term memory loss, I didn't remember them having cared for me. It was embarrassing, but they seemed to understand, and assisted with my memory if they could, while never questioning or making me feel as if something was wrong.

This time, I had many of the same staff, but because of my short-term memory loss, I didn't remember them having cared for me.

The cardiologist decided it was time to move to addressing the problem with which everything had begun: the cardiac arrest. The head trauma, as the most immediate danger, had taken precedence in my immediate care and surgical procedures. The cardiologist had scheduled an EP (electrophysiology) study two days earlier in hopes that it would give some answers to the sudden death incident that had caused me to collapse and ultimately undergo the head trauma injury and surgery. Everything had been put on hold until the bleeding from my brain was stopped and they could be sure I was stabilized.

Now it was time for a second set of experts to put in time trying to determine why my heart had suddenly stopped. Everyone knew I was not going to be released from the hospital until we had discussed definite options.

When the initial cardiac arrest occurred 12 years ago, the cardiologist in St. Louis who had been treating me for cardiomyopathy since the birth of my second daughter also ordered an EP (electro-physiology) study of my heart. The test is designed to determine whether an episode will reoccur if the heart is manipulated to mimic the deadly arrhythmia. The findings were inconclusive, and after a week's observation, I was sent home. There was no diagnosis, and the event was considered an unexplainable fluke that hopefully would never happen again. I accepted those words of wisdom and hoped they were right, and was determined to be thankful that I had survived and get on with life.

At that time, getting on with life meant that my family was in transition preparing to move to Orlando, Florida, to begin a new ministry with Campus Crusade for Christ. Our home and furniture had been sold and we had said many farewells to friends and family. Our emotions had been running high with anticipation for six months or more. My husband had already begun his new job and was staying with co-workers from the ministry while the girls and I stayed behind to sell our house. Since there was no known cause for the cardiac arrest, or at least they could not replicate the incident to find a solution, we were told not to make the cross country move for three months to allow me to return to driving and normal activities.

> *It was not until many years later that I fully appreciated how adversely an illness or accident can affect a child and an entire family.*

Within 30 days, I began to grow impatient and tried to convince my husband to shift the moving day closer, but we continued to heed the doctor's advice, and made the 1,200 mile move in September to an unknown city and unfamiliar people to begin a new adventure.

This time, after having lived through the ordeal once, I realized how foolish it had been to act as though nothing had happened. Our move and "new adventure" had been a horrible experience for our family and especially for our daughters, who had suffered a great deal of trauma from my collapse. We tried to ignore what had happened and use the hospital's less than helpful non-diagnosis as an excuse to chalk it up to coincidence, hoping it would not happen again. Our then-14-year-old daughter Abby had always been very close to the family and was somewhat of an introvert by nature. Because of her natural early teen insecurities and the relocation, she became less social, more fearful, and more protective of our relationship. April, our 10-year-old, felt guilty that she hadn't helped in some way, remembering having retreated into the bathroom when she witnessed everything happening and her sister frantically trying to save me.

It was not until many years later that I fully appreciated how adversely an illness or accident can affect a child and an entire family. In retrospect, we should have sought professional counseling to help us individually and as a family to discuss what had happened and how we could help each other talk through our feelings and determine any additional need for medical or professional help. At a minimum, my husband and I should have discussed the incident with our daughters and encouraged them to talk about their fears and ask questions to help them feel more secure. Instead, I think we wanted them not to have to think about or deal with the emotions surrounding what they had experienced, maybe because we thought the move was enough of an ordeal for them to handle at the time.

After that collapse 12 years earlier, I had shown normal ejection fraction levels (a measure of how much blood one's heart is pumping) at my cardiac check-ups and echocardiograms. I continued to take medication and saw my cardiologist annually. Now, I was lying in the hospital bed, more than a decade older in experience and in years, wondering what this EP testing might reveal about my heart. I also could not imagine how God would turn this for my good and His glory. I had already been told by the neurosurgeons that I was "a very lucky lady to be alive." The two of them examined my head daily where they had worked so feverishly to save my life, probing the incision where my metal plates had been

> *They were aware of the grim possibilities while also being pleased to see any progress...*

screwed into place. They were encouraged by indications of healing, but many times they would just smile and shake their heads.

I took those responses as a dose of realism. They were aware of the grim possibilities while also being pleased to see any progress suggesting success. Doctors and nurses monitored my stats and continued to check my improvement, but I knew the original problem had been my heart. The key was lying in the center of my chest. It had been seven days since my admittance into the hospital, and now I tried to ready myself for the following day of testing on my heart. Within minutes of the neurosurgeon's exit, the cardiologist entered to explain the electrophysiology (EP) study scheduled for the following day at 7:30 in the morning. She took time to give a detailed explanation of the test and what I would experience during the procedure, a description summed up in this information written for patients undergoing an EP study:

During an electrophysiology study, electrode catheters are guided into the chambers of the heart and at strategic places along its conduction system. Once in place, these electrodes record the electrical impulses of the heart and define the exact location of abnormal electrical activity. You will be instructed not to eat or drink anything after midnight prior to your procedure. Patients who are taking prescription medications are advised accordingly prior to their EP study.

You will be awake during the procedure; however, you will be given sedation to make you drowsy. Your heart rate, rhythm, and blood pressure will be continuously monitored.

The area where the sheath will be inserted will be numbed with a local anesthetic. While the sheath is being inserted you may feel slight pressure. The catheter is inserted through the sheath and threaded to the heart. The Electrophysiology Lab is equipped with special imaging equipment that allows the physician to view the catheter as it is threaded towards the heart. While the catheter is moving through your body you should feel no pain. The catheter is connected to an EKG machine so the electrical activity of the heart can be monitored internally. The electrophysiologist will then pace the heart by sending impulses through the catheter to several areas of the heart. The catheter and sheath are removed when the study is completed. Pressure will be placed on the sheath site, and once the bleeding has stopped, a dressing (bandage) will be applied.

Following the study, a nurse will continue to monitor your heart rate, blood pressure, pulse, and insertion site. You will be instructed to lie flat with your head slightly elevated at a 30-degree angle. A routine EP study will last for three to four hours. With the insertion site in your groin, you will be asked not to move your leg, since limiting the movement of your leg will help prevent bleeding. *(Cited: Electrophysiology Services www.humc.com/heart)*

> *I knew my health had taken a turn for the worse... but no one seemed to know why.*

As the cardiologist talked about the procedure and what they were hoping to detect, I hoped she was wrong, that my heart was strong, and that it all might have been a bad dream. But I was glad to have good medical care and knew I was surrounded by family and friends who loved and cared about me.

Throughout the evening before the scheduled EP study, I found myself drained and more lethargic. I had trouble staying awake and couldn't manage to eat my lunch or dinner. Several nurses who were taking regular readings on vitals noticed an increase in my body temperature, and a blood test later in the afternoon revealed an elevated white blood count. The following morning, the cardiologist came to my hospital room, but I couldn't rally as she began to talk with me about the scheduled procedure.

My husband approached the doctor with his concerns about my lethargy, elevated temperature and white blood cell count. I couldn't seem to make myself converse and stay awake for more than short responses to questions. I knew my health had taken a turn for the worse, and everyone echoed the same concerns, but no one seemed to know why. The IV fluids were increased and my husband began offering me sips of water. I welcomed the cool water on my tongue, but it was a chore to swallow. After observing my condition for a brief moment, the cardiologist immediately decided to postpone the EP study until my condition improved.

I lay in my hospital bed not knowing why I suddenly felt so ill and drained. A few days earlier, my energy level had increased and I had been talking with my family and a few friends who visited, but now that energy was gone. The room was silent as my husband sat at my bedside. God had not spoken audibly but I felt impressed to respond to an inner prompting in my spirit and I now needed to share with Rick what I thought He was telling me. I am always cautious about what or how I might say that God "spoke" to me because I realize that some people use that terminology very lightly, but that afternoon it was as if He gave me the strength to ask for help when I was at one of my weakest points.

I called for Rick in a soft voice and he bent down to the bed, not sure if I was even calling him, thinking I might still be sleeping. I told him I felt God wanted us to call the elders of the church and follow the teaching in the book of James, Chapter 5, on prayer. There had been countless people interceding on my behalf, almost from the instant my accident occurred. But I could not dismiss the feeling that I needed something in addition to those prayers, not that they had not been heard and answered. God had definitely responded in a miraculous way and had guided the hands of the surgeons and brought healing to my brain.

Upon hearing the passage from James suddenly run through my mind, I had known it was more than just a thought. Because of the brain injury, I had been unable to concentrate and bring many things to memory. I had been frustrated just a few days earlier that I couldn't even think of my ABCs, recall numbers, or put more than a three-word sentence together. But suddenly, when my husband bent to my bedside, I said to him, "Call the elders of the church." In an audible, succinct voice, I continued, "Is anyone of you sick? He should call the elders of the church to pray over him and anoint him with oil in the name of the Lord. And the prayer offered in faith will make the sick person well; the Lord will raise him up."

Rick stood and immediately looked a little puzzled because I hadn't had the ability to talk or eat throughout the day, and now he was hearing me quote an entire Bible passage. My eyes were still closed, but I repeated the request for him to call the church. Because we had been attending a new church for only about five months, he shared later that he wasn't sure if it would be the thing to do. Moreover, our former church had been a mega-church, so being personable with fellow members had been an issue for us in the past. When Rick asked who I wanted him to call, wanting to cover all bases I replied, "Call both churches," hoping this late in the day we might get a call from someone or at least be able to leave a voice mail.

To my surprise, within the hour, a pastor from our former church came into my room and greeted me with a smile that said he would be happy to pray for me. Taking my hand, he began to quote the James 5 passage I had quoted earlier. The pastor remained for a brief time, but I couldn't keep my eyes open or stay awake except for short periods of time. Rick said he had called both churches just as I had asked. He expected the pastor of our current fellowship to come later. By 7:30 in the evening, the sliding door to my neuro-trauma intensive care room opened.

"...call the elders of the church and let them pray..."

I opened my eyes slightly to recognize our pastor and then saw that he was followed by six men. Some I recognized from the few times we had been to the church, but others were strangers to me. Yet, I cannot describe the feeling of genuine love and overwhelming awareness of the spirit of God as they filed in, and as each approached my sickbed in meekness and humility.

The pastor began by telling me that the men had met before coming to the hospital to pray and confess their sins in keeping with the Word of God. He took my badly bruised hand and grasped the small, cylindrical vial of oil. As he softly recited the passage, James 5:14-16, he spoke with reverence and in complete confidence that the power was in the One who was hearing the prayer, not in the one speaking it. He placed the light, smooth oil on my forehead and hand as he recited, *"Is anyone among you sick? Let him call for the elders of the church and let them pray over him, anointing him with oil in the name of the Lord. And the prayer of faith will save the one who is sick, and the Lord will raise him up. And if he has committed sins, he will be forgiven. Therefore, confess your sins to one another and pray for one another,* that you may be healed. The prayer of a righteous person has great power as it is working. " (ESV)

> *The prayers lasted in total not more than fifteen minutes, but their impact will last lifetimes, and possibly throughout eternity.*

Then, the other men took turns in offering prayers for my health, healing and care. I had heard of people who had been "prayed over," but had never experienced it personally, and probably would have formerly considered it too "charismatic" for my comfort level. There was nothing in me now that felt strange because I knew God had impressed upon my heart to ask for this prayer as an act of faith.

I know the praying had a huge impact on my spiritual life, but I also know that it had to have had an affect on our older daughter, Abby, who at the time was standing near the back of the room. My husband stood near my feet and the pastor by my head with the others encircling my hospital bed. This group of elders who had gathered around my sick bed clearly took the task seriously, and they prayed earnestly. The prayers lasted in total not more than fifteen minutes, but their impact will last lifetimes, and possibly throughout eternity, as people's lives are changed or brought closer to God.

The group filed out of the hospital room without talking. I wish I could tell you I leaped from the bed performing an Irish jig and the fever was immediately gone, but the truth is, I wasn't really thinking about the fever and infection. I lay flat on the hard hospital mattress with tubes, needles and wires running from several parts of my broken and bruised body, but amazingly, the thought of the sickness was not foremost in my mind. Rather, there was a satisfying sense of peace and tranquility that permeated my mind and relaxed my body. Another Bible passage, Philippians 4:4-7, came to mind: *"Rejoice in the Lord always; again I will say, Rejoice. Let your reasonableness be known to everyone. The Lord is at hand; do not be anxious about anything, but in every- thing by prayer and supplication with thanksgiving let your requests be made known to God. And the peace of God, which surpasses all understanding, will guard your hearts and your minds in Christ Jesus."* (ESV)

My natural instinct would have been to want a story that turned out like that of the blind man who had his eyesight restored, or of Lazarus being raised from the dead with a shout from the Lord to "come forth," or even of Peter's mother-in-law, who was touched by Jesus and was instantly healed of her fever. Instead, I immediately had a sense of overwhelming peace. For me, that rest and assurance were themselves a miracle, given my usual got-to-have-it-now-and-deliver-it-with-a-wow attitude.

I drifted off to sleep shortly after the prayer and felt the nurse make her rounds to draw blood, prick my finger and inject me with steroids. She took routine vitals and I heard her whisper to my husband, who was still propped up in the guest chair, "Her fever is down." The following day, I began to rally, with fluids and ice chips helping to bring the temperature down even more. Trying to find the root of the infection proved to be a guessing game, as experts concluded I had a urinary tract infection due to the length of time the original catheter had been in place. It was removed and I was rescheduled the following morning for the Cardiac Electrophysiology Study.

Two Moms: One Forgotten, One Forgetting

...you whom I have upheld since you were
conceived, and have carried since your birth.
Even to your old age and gray hairs I am
he, I am he who will sustain you.
I have made you and I will carry you; I will
sustain you and I will rescue you.
Isaiah 46:3-4

The prep time leading up to the early morning procedure was intense followed by the cardiac team wheel-
ing me down the corridor toward the cardiac catheter lab
and into the blinding white overhead lights and sterile, frigid
environment. Robed in sterile gowns, the cardiac professionals talked to me, trying to make the setting as comfortable as
possible. I remembered the first time I had the test, my groin

was extremely sore and tender as I lay with a small sandbag pressing against the artery. I had specific instructions not to move after the procedure. The team of nurses described the sensations I might expect, given that the test would be performed as much as possible without anesthesia so I could be somewhat alert. They gave me a drug through the IV to relax me during the time when my heart would be manipulated electronically in an effort to reenact the cardiac arrest by inducing extremes of the normal rhythm.

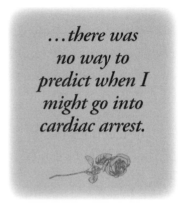

...there was no way to predict when I might go into cardiac arrest.

Once everything was in place, the cardiac team began by racing my heart and then slowing it to a below-average rate. I became very alert at this time, and a nurse rushed to my side to assure me the procedure was almost finished. Throughout the four hours of electronic manipulation, my heart received a workout, but it functioned without failure or incident. That was a good thing, but it meant the electrophysiology study team had been unable to recreate what had happened to me just days earlier that had caused me to collapse.

I had heard that evaluation 12 years earlier: an unfortunate occurrence, but an isolated incident. The doctors were unsure why the cardiac arrest had happened, but hopefully it would never happen again. Based on the EP study findings, there was no way to predict when I might go into cardiac arrest. My current cardiologist expressed her determination that she would do everything she could to prevent another episode like the one that almost took my life. She decided to implant a combination cardiac pacemaker/defibrillator device in my chest. Because I had experienced two cardiac arrests brought on by arrhythmias, I was a good candidate for the device.

When I was returned to my hospital room in the NICU, both legs were held down by weights to keep me from moving them. The dual device was implanted following the electrophysiology procedure. It was a tedious operation requiring an incision in my shoulder near the collarbone to place the device beneath the muscle. The electrophysiologist strategically attached electrodes into the heart muscle before implanting the device and closing the incision.

Initially, the cardiologist had made two attempts at inserting the catheter to access an artery during the testing. The catheter that had caused the urinary tract infection had been removed before the procedure but another had taken its place. My left arm, shoulder and chest were immobilized following the implantation of the defibrillator and would be for some time. My body was sore and exhausted. I felt as if I'd run a marathon, and as far as my heart was concerned, I had. But no one was handing out gold medals or asking for a victory speech. At that point, I suppose I felt that being alive was a victory and definitely worth more than a gold medal.

After observing my progress the following day, my cardiologist decided I would stay another day and then be released on Sunday. That was the best news my family and I had heard in almost two weeks. My husband had sat in the chair near my bed for so long, I wasn't sure he would be able to straighten up. But he jumped to his feet when nurses began preparing me for another move to the cardiac care unit for one final day before discharging me to send me home.

It was a strange feeling when the nurses who had cared for me for so long, who had bathed me and attended to my needs, came to my room to say our good-byes. Some gave hugs and well wishes and others just smiled, knowing that their work had not been for nothing. They were happy to see me able to recover and go home. I envisioned going back to the hospital after my recovery to visit them after I had grown back my hair, could walk without a limp, and had a face without bruised, black eyes. I was sure they often had patients they connected with, especially after long stays on the trauma floor. Undoubtedly those who work in the neuro-trauma intensive care unit see fewer patients who have a full recovery or even survive. We said our good-byes, and a nurse wheeled me to the cardiac floor and away from eleven days in intensive care.

I remembered the terrible experience earlier in the week when I had been transferred prematurely to the cardiac floor. I hoped this time would be without incident, and the brief stay before being released to go home would be uneventful. When we came into the semi-private room, the bed adjacent to mine had the curtain closed. I could hear an elderly woman as she labored to breathe.

After the nurses on the floor had introduced themselves and taken the necessary vital signs, I saw each of them make their way to the bed next to mine. Since it was mid-morning, I was surprised to hear the lady continuing to sleep. Later, when lunch was brought, she still didn't rouse. As nurses tried to wake her or inquire about her need for assistance, the woman often snapped at them with slurred speech, telling them to "go away" or "get out of here." Some of the younger nurses responded by exiting the room quickly, and many just peeked their heads in throughout the day to make sure she was breathing, while trying not to stir the sleeping patient.

Some of the more seasoned nurses knew what they needed to do, ignored the woman's gruff manner, and proceeded to attend to her needs. One of the younger male nurses treated her with more kindness than the rest. He would not only look in on her, but went the extra mile to talk to her as if she were a relative or friend. When her lunch had sat for a while and was getting cold, he brought the food, put it on her tray and pushed it closer to her bed. He asked her if she needed some help eating or wanted to be fed. She replied, "No, leave me alone. I don't want it."

He tried to reason with her by telling her that she needed to eat for her strength and that he would leave the tray there in case she changed her mind. She raised her voice and said, "No, no. Get out of here!" The nurse looked at me as he was leaving the room, shaking his head and smiling as if to say, "You just keep watching. She'll eat." Within a few minutes after he exited the room, I heard slurping and munching. My husband and I smiled at each other and shrugged in amazement.

The remainder of the day brought various friends of our family wanting to visit, since they hadn't had the opportunity in the ICU. Throughout the day as people talked and laughed, I caught myself listening for the mysterious lady behind the curtain. I could hear her breathing and sometimes coughing. When the visitors had left and my dinner tray had been taken, I was aware that the woman's food was still sitting far from her bed and reach. The attendant asked if she was finished, but there was no answer. When he repeated his question louder, the patient snarled in a raspy voice, "No, no, leave it," and he quickly moved the tray closer to the hungry patient. I envisioned the animal-like frantic chomping and gobbling that followed coming from a starved homeless person.

Suddenly, the chewing stopped and a long breath began with a harsh choking and cough. I feared she might be in danger and broke the silence: "Ma'am, are you okay? Ma'am, do you need me to call the nurse?" The coughing continued but I couldn't move from my bed because of the catheters and remaining tubes still attached to my body. Pressing the nurse call button, I was filled with concern for the frail little lady who lay within four feet of my bed, but whom I had never met. Before the nurse's station had a chance to pick up the call, I heard relief come as her gagging dislodged the offending bite and she expelled it with a loud spit. A nurse came on the speaker asking what was needed and I simply explained that the woman in the next bed could use some help.

When the nurse, one of those I recognized as having years of nursing experience, arrived at the door of the room and realized who she was dealing with, I saw her take a deep breath before entering. Her stride slowed as she hesitantly approached the woman's bedside. Greeting the patient, she commented on the mess and joked about her getting more on the outside of her body than the inside. Shortly afterwards, the nurse called for an aide and another set of hands. An argument ensued between the patient and workers as the nurses tried to reason with the woman about needing to change her soiled hospital gown and sheets. I could hear the woman's defiant complaints: "Leave me alone! Don't bother me! Get away from me!" Her words were slurred and raspy, but nevertheless troubling as both parties battled the disease of sickness, sadness and frailty, everyone struggling with the fact that life often changes a person to act and react in ways contrary to their personality and character.

...life often changes a person to act and react in ways contrary to their personality and character.

After several minutes, the wrestling match was brought to a close and the great exchange was completed. The exhausted nurses turned to leave the room. The original nurse who had been attending the woman stopped near the end of the curtain that bordered our individual patient space. The nurse's face turned toward the lady with a pleasant smile, and her voice softened as if she were talking to her own mother. She slowly and simply said, "Mrs. C., your daughter called today and she hopes to be able to come see you soon." Pausing, the nurse, who had formerly been almost military in her demeanor, continued, "She said to tell you that she loves you."

The nurse waited for a moment, but when no response came, she turned to leave the room to continue her duties. Catching my eye, she quickly looked down at the glossy blue tiled floor and ran her finger under her nose with a sniff. I lay in my bed, thinking about what kind of daughter the woman had or if she had other family members. Within seconds, I could hear her breathing become heavy as she fell into a deep sleep. I thought of my own mother and the times she had been by my side in the past, and about the present circumstances that prevented her from being able to be with me now and how I missed her.

I thought of my own mother... and how I missed her.

The last time I had seen my mother was three months earlier at her home on the farm where she and my father lived. Thoughts and memories of her had flooded my mind as we made the six-hour trip to see them. Trips had become increasingly more difficult over the past few years as Alzheimer's disease changed my mother into a stranger, even though she remained capable of independently caring for herself for the most part. Family gatherings or overnight trips seemed to make her agitated and anxious, so we tried to help her remain calm and peaceful.

We had dealt with the disease with my grandmother when she was in her early 80s. She died from complications of the disease that ended in a fall and broken hip that proved to be fatal four years after her diagnosis. My grandmother's father also struggled with and later succumbed to the disease before Alzheimer's was recognized and diagnosed as such. He was institutionalized on several occasions before his death because of his misunderstood behavior and illness.

My mother began showing signs of personality changes and mild confusion at age 62, the same year my grandmother died. She was considering early retirement, and we thought the stress from work and caring for my grandmother was taking its toll on Mom, and that she would eventually improve. Within a year of my grandmother's death, however, my mother was diagnosed with beginning stages of Alzheimer's.

We kept that news a secret from her for fear it would adversely affect her. Over the next 2-3 years, she grew more dependent on my father, and became unable to tolerate larger family gatherings, which were both out of character for Mom. We began having those events at the home of my brother and sister-in-law, who lived in the same town. The past 3-5 years had taken her ability to speak and communicate, but even with the changes, I still looked forward to "going home."

On that last visit home, the miles leading up to the one-lane gravel road elicited in me a combination of excitement and familiarity. Turning into the narrow private lane leading to the red brick farmhouse and bright crimson barn always created a sense of serenity in my soul. It was much like the feeling a child has when returning home from school at the end of a long, hard day; there was a familiar ease in knowing and being known. The drive ended with a pair of black and tan beagles announcing our arrival.

No one came to welcome us as had been the custom in the past, but as we turned the door handle to let ourselves in, I saw her sitting on the green tweed sofa with her back to the door. The side door where we entered allowed her to see us as we stepped inside, but she made no movement to acknowledge the sound. We walked into the house and greeted my dad. As usual, he was sitting at the kitchen snack bar with a cup of black coffee, surrounded by a halo of cigarette smoke in front of an overflowing ashtray. He greeted us with soft, somber eyes and asked how our trip had been, and if we had run into any rain.

...his eyes were no longer pools of joy but windows into his grieving soul.

My father is a gentle rotund man with the rough, careworn skin of a seasoned farmer. His most prominent feature has always been his kind, soft, deep blue eyes. Many times I had seen them sparkle with life, especially at the sight of my mother. But that day, I saw him turn his gaze toward the woman he had cherished for more than 50 years and his eyes were no longer pools of joy but windows into his grieving soul.

My mother didn't acknowledge that anyone was near her, so I was cautious not to startle or surprise her. Nervous, I walked softly over to where she was perched on the edge of the couch and sat next to her. I was careful not to disturb her neatly folded and stacked rows of washcloths and various other items that she seemed to derive comfort in organizing. She continued her folding as I sat near her, uninterrupted by my presence and unaware that we had come for a visit. I called her name and she looked up at me with a big smile. She pulled me close and hugged me in a tight, unyielding grip. She kissed my cheek and continued to hold onto my arm. We embraced for a long time as she tried to speak, but no intelligible words came.

We embraced for a long time as she tried to speak, but no intelligible words came.

For so many years, I had heard her speak on all sorts of topics, giving her opinion or relating her experience on everything from recipes, gardening, and crafts to the grandkids, students at school, family and friends, but I longed for another chance to sit and talk about anything or nothing.

After we had been sitting for some time, my dad decided to go outside to check on the cattle on his ATV. The two of us sat in silence as she continued to pat and caress my hand. For the first time, I looked deep into her eyes and held her face in both of my hands. "Mom," I queried, "What are you thinking? Please help me to know where you've gone and how to get you back." She looked at me and the corners of her mouth went up but her eyes were hauntingly gray and empty. They had always been like beautiful deep pools of azure, different in shape and hue from my father's.

Because I have a different biological father than my brother

I knew he was trying to make it easier for me to go, but I hoped he was wrong. And I knew that even if she did forget, I never would.

and sister, I was born with big brown eyes and dark hair. As a child I had desperately wanted the same blue eyes so many in my family had, but specifically I wanted eyes like my mom's. Over the past few years, I saw her bright blue eyes fade to pale shadows of gray. The vibrant life that had danced and been reflected in them for so long was losing its essence and spirit.

Soon, her attention returned to the stacks of individual sheets of toilet paper lying in front of her on the oval coffee table. Picking up a sheet, she painstakingly folded the square sheet of two-ply tissue, first into a rectangle and then into a perfect square while holding it gingerly on her lap. Pointing to her neatly stacked work, she tried to talk, but became frustrated in her effort to communicate. "N-n-n-n-n, no, no honey," she stammered, as she struggled to show her accomplishment to me. I tried to reply in a positive way, but she turned from me as if I didn't exist or she didn't know who I was. Taking my hand that she had clutched and stroked earlier, she threw it back into my lap in an agitated way. She motioned to me and said, "No, n-n-n-n-n no, honey, g-g-g-g-g go." She rose, took my hand, and led me toward the door. I knew I hadn't done anything wrong but it was time to go. I wished we could have stayed longer, but I didn't want to upset her for any reason and I was glad for what time I had spent with her.

When I told my dad what had happened, he tried to encourage me, saying, "Don't think anything of it. She won't even remember when you leave." I knew he was trying to make it easier for me to go, but I hoped he was wrong. And I knew that even if she did forget, I never would.

As with most visits, the drive home was difficult as I attempted to reconcile myself to my mom's condition. I had envisioned my mom and myself enjoying our adult lives together, especially when Rick and I had moved back to the area after living 1,200 miles away for almost five years. But, as with so much of life, these things are unpredictable, and always the days and the time we have to spend with loved ones and friends are much too short. Knowing this, I've tried to practice my mother's advice to give flowers to the living not only as it applies to flowers, but as it relates to time, energy and resources that can have an impact on my relationships now. I'm sure I haven't always spent that time wisely, and when I think of all the things I wish I had said to Mom, I conclude the problem is that there isn't enough time to say the things that matter when you think it may be your last opportunity to do so.

Suddenly, the woman next to my bed began to cough again and I was brought back to the reality of my hospital room. Sometimes, thinking about my collapse and all that had happened just 12 days earlier, I wasn't sure if I could fully grasp the scope of events and where I was at that moment. Aside from my own situation, I wondered whether the older lady's daughter was thinking of her and what kind of relationship they had – whether the nurse had truly been relaying a message or just trying to make her patient feel better. I hoped for both their sakes that they had learned to appreciate the gift of life and family.

Since I had never met "Mrs. C.," I didn't know her or have any preconceived ideas about her or her family. The night nurses came into the room to check vital signs for the last time on what was, for me, my last night in the hospital. I felt like a person who was being released from jail, not that I would know exactly how that felt. But I had seen movies about prisoners who were freed and immediately looked at the outside world as they never had before, with a renewed appreciation for life; the sky was bluer, the grass greener, and the air sweeter.

For me, there was certainly an excitement about making plans to get back to my normal way of life. But as I listened to Mrs. C. and watched another new patient being wheeled into the room next door, I thought of how different "normal" is for everyone. For me, it was our immediate family, my husband, our younger daughter, our granddaughter, and for the time being while she stayed to help in my recovery, our older daughter. The thoughts of those who had been a big part of my life and were now gone filled my mind with memories of days spent with them and times we had shared.

I drifted off to sleep between interruptions from nurses. I listened to the sounds of sleeping and working going on simultaneously. I peered at my husband, who finally had a cot to sleep on at the foot of my bed, and he appeared to be at rest.

Finally a nurse came in and flipped on the bright light over our beds, waking Mrs. C. and ending my slumber party.

It was morning, albeit very early in the morning, but I felt like a schoolgirl getting ready for a party as I contemplated going home. It would be wonderful – no more IVs, steroid shots, finger sticks, catheters, and unidentifiable food or smells. I knew a full recovery was still a long way off, but I knew I could gain strength and stamina in the comfort of my home. In my way of thinking, it was 6 a.m., and I expected to be home by lunchtime at the latest.

Still facing several physical limitations, I waited patiently for the nurses to dress me after breakfast. Doctors came in to give me the once-over and their blessing, or at least to sign the release forms. Since it was Sunday, the doctors on call had never seen me, so they put me through the rigors of proving I could stand, walk, and communicate before checking my incision where the defibrillator had been implanted.

Okay, I was more than ready as lunchtime arrived and I realized the day was being wasted. Picking at my food and growing tired from my waning sleep and continuing weakness, I reclined in my bed, pushed the tray away and prayed for patience but hoped for expediency. At 5 p.m., my frustration became evident and my husband approached a nurse. Apparently the doctor who had seen me during the earlier morning shift was supposed to have released me, but had neglected to sign my paperwork.

After a few calls and another hour, the nurse finally came in to help me into the wheelchair to escort me to our car. Mrs. C. was still sleeping; her heavy rhythmic breathing continued. I noted the flurry of activity at the nurses' desk as we passed. Everyone was busy with their schedules and routines as they went about their business. Two of the nurses took a moment to wave good-bye and send me home with well wishes.

PART TWO

Do not take lightly the value and brevity of life. You have one life to live and one life to give. Make sure that the thing that you're giving your life for will last beyond this short span of earthly living.

—unknown

There's No Place Like Home

Lord, you establish peace for us; all that we have accomplished you have done for us. Isaiah 26:12

Our daughter Abby stayed by my side as we waited with the attendant for Rick to bring the car to the hospital portico to pick us up and take us home. As we had passed the coffee shop and gift store I remembered the aroma of coffee beans brewing filling the entry. Three years earlier we had driven to the same hospital on three occasions before they admitted our daughter April to the maternity floor, and we had subsequently welcomed our beautiful baby grand-daughter, Ella, into this world. After bringing the two of them home from the hospital, we found that the only brand of pacifier the baby would use was the one given to her at the hospital, which was available only at the gift shop or online.

So we made a quick trip to buy all the available binkies for emergencies.

My familiar black car drove up to the triple automatic entrance doors, and the attendant moved me up, activating the door sensor. The brilliant foyer lights were blinding to my sensitive eyes and the afternoon air was brisk and chilly. It was still daylight, but the overcast sky made it appear to be much later in the evening. My husband lifted me into the car's passenger seat as carefully as if I might break. Given my multiple injuries, he found it a difficult and exacting chore to place the seatbelt in a suitable manner around my head, chest and leg. I couldn't believe that the energy was already escaping my body and we hadn't even started the drive home.

As we pulled onto the highway, I was in awe of the brilliant colors of the green grass and brightly colored vehicles that dotted our path. I felt as excited as if I were on an adventure as we sat at the red light waiting to race toward our goal. As we passed a Braum's ice cream shop, a McDonald's restaurant, and several convenience stores, I thought of the trips we had made in the past that created the memories of our everyday, fast-paced, hectic lives, and of the celebrations and rewards for our children when they were young.

Continuing on the road that turned toward the familiar lake where I regularly looked forward to seeing the big, gray heron, I looked toward the buoy where she perched herself every morning. The wind whipped the water to create ripples as the treetops swayed in our direction. Daylight was dimming and I could feel myself becoming tense. My reduced sense of depth perception and blurred vision made it difficult for me to trust the vehicles around us as we continued the drive, and my discomfort grew. Rick looked over at me, put his hand on mine and said, "I am so glad to be taking you home."

"Me, too," I said, and forced a smile. But although the thought was awkward, given how much I had wanted to go home, I suddenly wondered if I had left the hospital too soon. Was I really ready? My thoughts started to race as panic and fear began to terrorize my mind. I wondered what would happen if I had another cardiac arrest. Who would be there to resuscitate me? What if I collapsed, hit my head and no one was there to help me? What if something happened at night while everyone was asleep?

The fear continued and I could feel the hot tears welling up in my eyes and blocking my throat as I tried to swallow.

The fear continued and I could feel the hot tears welling up in my eyes and blocking my throat as I tried to swallow. My husband saw the fear in my face and wondered if I was in pain, or what else might have caused the change in attitude. I couldn't put my feelings into words, but I was suddenly petrified and truly regretted leaving the perceived security of the hospital. I wished I was back where I could be monitored.

Even as I was bombarded with unreasonable thoughts,

I couldn't seem to remain calm. It all sounded crazy, even to me, but my fear-driven anxiety would not allow me to reason and think rationally. We drove another mile or two, then turned onto a residential roadway and approached a familiar farmhouse. Then I saw them. It was the miniature ponies I had tried to tell everyone about while I was in the hospital, and no one would believe me. I burst into tears as I looked at all the furry animals running and kicking up their heels along the roadside. There were more than a dozen of them, running along the electric fence as if to welcome me back home to the neighborhood.

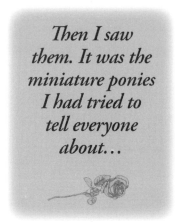

Then I saw them. It was the miniature ponies I had tried to tell everyone about...

Part of me cried because I knew what I had told the nurses had not been totally due to hallucinations, although I knew my mind had been confused – the dream about the ponies had in fact been based in part on my real-life experience. I wanted to take a picture of the horses and send it to the nurse I had told about the ponies while in the hospital, the one who didn't believe me. Then I could say, "See, I told you that there are miniature ponies near my house. I wasn't imagining them and I'm not crazy!"

Of course, my thoughts immediately went to the feelings of foolishness I had felt when the nurse in the neuro-intensive care unit had been insensitive about my confusion when

I tried to relate to her my dream about the ponies, and the horrible nightmares and hallucinations that had followed. My mind flashed back to clinching the sheet in my fist, trying desperately to prove that I hadn't lost my mind. The tears continued to flow and Rick attempted to comfort me and reason with me as I relived the event. He knew that within minutes we would arrive at our home with our daughters and granddaughter anxiously waiting to greet us, and we wouldn't want them to see me in this state.

We drove slowly and my husband kept talking. His soft, kind, confident voice was soothing and comforting. I knew the words he said were true, but I found it hard to find reassurance away from the medical facility and trained professionals who had worked so hard to save and preserve my life. The truth was that I had not only lived through the cardiac arrest, head trauma and surgery, the defibrillator implant and 12 days of intensive care treatment and observation, but I was getting stronger everyday and I was alive and well. I knew, of course, that it was God who had permitted me to live and had orchestrated everything, from the staff person at work who had resuscitated me to the medical teams and professionals who had performed life-saving surgeries and given life-sustaining treatments.

God is the Great Physician and I give Him all the glory for the healing, but the doctors and nurses get the paychecks. I am forever grateful for their labor, sacrifice, and commitment as a team working in conjunction with Him. It is a wise doctor who admits his or her humanity and limitations. I have a great deal of respect for my medical caregivers' compassion, skill and knowledge, but also realize their humanity as finite beings with limited abilities.

We soon topped the hill, coming in sight of our neighborhood and home. I immediately thought of the nightly bedtime story that I would tell my granddaughter each evening as we connected at the end of the day. Slipping on her cute little princess jammies, hopping into bed and pulling the blanket to her chin, she would look at me with wide eyes full of anticipation, even though she had heard the story every night for more than a year. My eyebrows would arch and my voice tone changed to a whisper as I transformed into a storyteller spinning her magical yarn.

"Once upon a time, there was a little girl named Ella who lived in a beautiful red brick house at the top of a very steep, high hill. She lived with her mommy, her poppy and her nana, who loved her so very much. Every day, Ella would play with her two puppy dogs, one named Sammy and the other named Sophie. And that little girl had the longest, most beautiful hair in the world…" The story eventually told of the day's events or fun experiences with the family or friends, and of course it would end in the assurance that she lived "happily ever after." Sometimes, I would attempt to change or alter the beginning of the story to see if she was listening or was ready for something new, but she would always correct me to make sure that certain important parts were in place, as if to reassure her of the constant care and stability she needed and relied on.

On that day, I felt like that little girl who needed all those same things, and as the garage door lifted it revealed just that assurance, in the faces of my family standing expectantly, awaiting my return. I was not only reminded of their love, but I remembered why my favorite movie of all time was "The Wizard of Oz": because there really is "no place like home." I know that sounds corny and cliché, but it is true. No one knows you or accepts you as readily and completely as your family. As soon as the door to the house opened, three smiling faces appeared, and I saw open arms, offer-

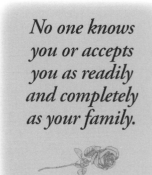

No one knows you or accepts you as readily and completely as your family.

ing welcoming hugs and kisses. I wondered if I was having another dream, but if I was, I wanted to continue it for as long as possible.

The house was dimly but beautifully lit with candles producing sweet aromas of warm sugar cookies and a hint of hazelnut. I secretly wondered if they hadn't had time to clean and wanted to hide the clutter and dirt, but I didn't really care. It was nice to see them working together as a team to make everything nice for me. They smiled, and April proudly took me by the hand and escorted me as the others followed me into the bedroom and bathroom where more candles awaited us, along with new matching bath towels, lotions and soaps, creating a spa-like atmosphere. In the background, peaceful, relaxing sounds of ocean waves filled the air. The girls' eyes lit up when they saw how pleased I was, and how grateful for the time and

...everyday life has a way of stealing that commitment and expression...

thoughtfulness they had put into making things special. I wanted to savor this moment as a time when we had all come together as a family and truly had hearts of love and appreciation for one another.

I knew, of course, that we cared for one another and would do anything for each other, but everyday life has a way of stealing that commitment and expression, although we know we should not allow that to happen. I hoped that after the candles had gone out, the new towels were soiled and dirty, and the channel had been switched from soothing spa sounds to chatter around the dinner table, that we would never forget how fortunate we are to have one another.

The first night at home sleeping in my own bed, I tossed and turned to find a comfortable position. Remarkably, I found myself searching for the controls to raise or lower my head and legs. On a positive note, there were no bright lights and interruptions for blood drawing; I would say it had been a good trade-off. Although I surrounded myself with fluffy pillows to shield me from my husband's flailing arms in the middle of the night, there was still a lot of discomfort from my incisions and the device implanted in my chest. I had been told that the defibrillator was approximately the size of a matchbox and weighed about six ounces. However, the left side of my chest would beg to differ.

The doctors tried to disguise the device by placing it under and supporting it with muscle, but since weightlifting has never been a priority for me, that method didn't work so well. It felt much like being given a hospital gown to wear. After wrapping the gray-blue bolt of material resembling that of a shop towel around my body three times, I usually gave up and tucked the ends into an opening. The concept was the same, only this time the exaggerated medical device left a nasty four-inch scar and filled the entire cavity of the left side of my chest. Every night in the next few days when I would lie down, I would need help just to rise from the bed to go to the bathroom.

Propping my arm up and trying to remain on my back seemed like an impossible task, or at least very uncomfortable, and kept the nights from becoming a time of peace, rest and sleep. Often I would lie embedded between the two pillows, listening for the sound of my heart. I wondered if it was aware of the mechanical guardian that was poised to jolt it if it failed to function. It felt strange to have the implanted sentinel, but a part of me was comforted knowing modern medicine had provided some peace of mind to those of us with life-threatening or I should say, life-robbing arrhythmias. I was certainly not relying on this hunk of metal and electrodes attached to my heart to keep me on this earth a second longer than God intended, but I had to admit that I was intensely glad to be alive, and I cherished being home with my family.

Because I am a research enthusiast, in the days that followed I wanted to find out more about cardiac arrest,

Each year, more than 250,000 people in the United States die from sudden cardiac arrest.

especially when the news soon after I came home showcased a young woman, famous in the movie industry, who had died after a similar occurrence in her home. I have since learned that the statistics on sudden cardiac arrest are staggering. The following information, which comes from such resources as the Centers for Disease Control and Prevention and the American Heart Association, was eye opening:

- Each year, more than 250,000 people in the United States die from sudden cardiac arrest. Most have no warning or symptoms and no hope of help of resuscitation from someone nearby to perform CPR or receive medical attention. Most have no prior cardiac health issues or prior heath problems.
- Sudden Cardiac Arrest (SCA) is a leading cause of death among adults over the age of 40.
- Approximately 10 percent of SCA events occur among people less than 40 years of age.
- More people die each year from SCA than the number who die from colorectal cancer, breast cancer, prostate cancer, auto accidents, AIDS, firearms, and house fires combined.
- Fewer than one-third of cardiac arrest victims receive CPR.

- Effective CPR can double or triple survival rates.
- On average, only one out of 15 SCA victims survives when a defibrillator is not onsite. CPR alone cannot save someone in Sudden Cardiac Arrest.
- If defibrillation occurs within 1 minute there is a 90% chance of survival. Survival rates drop by 10 percent for each minute of delay.
- Fewer than one percent of out-of-hospital sudden cardiac arrest victims survive because defibrillation does not begin early enough and CPR is not always given.
- Typical 911 response time is between 11 and 16 minutes. It is higher in rural and volunteer responder areas.

Often the fatalities are healthy athletes and young adults.

- A recent AHA survey shows few Americans are confident they could actually perform CPR and use an AED to help save a life in an emergency cardiac situation.

I'm sure this is not a new phenomenon, but the medical community and even media have finally begun to give it more attention. Often the fatalities are healthy athletes and young adults. When I was a young child, I remember hearing about people in our town who were found dead in their beds or had been napping and never woke up, but they were mostly elderly people, or those who had experienced prior heart problems. It was unheard of for a young person to collapse from cardiac arrest.

I had always been very active and athletic, playing competitive team sports in volleyball, softball and racquetball. I loved the outdoors and had worked on our family farm through my late teens while continuing to lead an active lifestyle as an adult and remaining conscious about my eating habits and vitamin supplements. The morning of my collapse, like the majority of sudden cardiac attack victims, I had experienced no sickness or warning to prompt any concern.

The Long and Winding Abby Road

Abby, who had been living in Pennsylvania for the past year, continued to stay with us after my hospital release to help me as I recovered. The relationship had been strained over the past four years and a deep hurt remained, but I continued to long for a restored bond with her. We had been very close through her adolescent years. She was my first child and I had built my life around her.

As a young girl, she had struggled with social acceptance, but excelled in several areas, especially in English composition, literature, track and gymnastics. She had a few friends from church and our home school support group, but was naturally a one-on-one person who preferred personal relationships rather than large crowds of people. At age 23, after moving out of our home and into her own apartment, Abby met and dated a man who had sold her a used car, literally. When they had been dating only a few months, my husband and I discovered that there was not only a 12-year age difference, divorce in his past, and three children from a previous marriage, but that he showed no interest in spiritual matters and proved to be a negative influence on our daughter.

Given Abby's Christian background, we thought the relationship would surely end because of disinterest on her part, and in the surety that she could not yoke herself with an unbeliever. In our minds, there could be no future with him; they were light years apart in goals, interests, lifestyles and experiences. After we had met the man twice, the way he behaved confirmed our fears, and we realized the relationship between the two of them was dangerously unhealthy.

Abby knew that we could not, with a clear conscience, encourage her decision to pursue any involvement with this man. She withdrew from us and ultimately rebelled by secretly marrying him while her sister, father, and I were on a mission trip in Mexico. When we returned and learned what had taken place, our lives and relationship with our daughter changed forever.

The strain ran through our immediate and extended family with well-meaning relatives struggling to lend support in a situation that could not be explained. I couldn't begin to imagine the lifelong hurt and disappointment her decision would cause, and where there had once been a closer than average relationship, she had suddenly disappeared from our lives. At certain times of the year, she would make limited contact and there would be some progress in the strained relationship. Often the positives were followed by a word or conversation leading to greater regression.

I knew Abby had been working and staying in St. Louis for a month leading up to my collapse, but before she had driven back from Pennsylvania, we had experienced a major breakdown on the phone and were both left with additional scars from hurtful words and unresolved frustration. A day never passed that I didn't long for a relationship with her and grieve the loss of our close bond.

> *A day never passed that I didn't long for a relationship with her and grieve the loss of our close bond.*

Following the year after her marriage and our breakdown, I moved into what I thought was survival mode and became engrossed in my work at the non-profit medical clinic where I managed the client services department that mentored young girls and their families facing crisis pregnancies. The morning I woke up from having the emergency head trauma surgery in the hospital, I struggled with blurred vision and confusion, but Abby's was one of the first faces I recognized. Her small, petite frame was a hazy silhouette standing next to my bed. Unsure where I was exactly, I wondered if I was dreaming, but when I closed my eyes, I felt her thin hands and fingers stroke mine. Her hands were tiny, soft and smooth, like a child's. She was soft-spoken and sensitive to the seriousness of the situation, unlike in our last conversation, in which our emotions had erupted into a verbal warfare of the heart.

I was relieved to have Abby stay with us for a period of time after the hospital stay came to an end. I think everyone, except me, realized that coming home didn't mean that I was fully recovered. Just as the emotional drive home had been a reminder that I had far to go in the healing process, bedtime reminded me that physical and emotional pain rear their ugly heads at the midnight hour. My nights were often full of fearful moments, wondering if my heart might stop without warning as it had done before, with bouts of restless sleep and irritation from the broken ankle, surgical scars, and cardiac device.

...bedtime reminded me that physical and emotional pain rear their ugly heads at the midnight hour.

Because Abby was accustomed to sleeping in, sometimes until 11 o'clock or later, I had often been fully awake for five or six hours by the time she arose. She would offer to cook breakfast and serve me hot tea with milk and sugar. I often thought of the countless tea parties we had hosted with her Cabbage Patch, Babysitter, and Barbie dolls when she was a little girl. Careful to clasp the rare molded plastic china cups with precision and point our pinkies, we would daintily sip our orange pekoe tea, sitting as proper young ladies at the royal blue and white Little Tykes table and chairs. We had such fun playing and pretending in her world of genuine innocence and purity.

Now, when Abby knelt to stir my cup of tea and place it on the nightstand next to my bed, I noticed a few light facial lines etched into her forehead and flanking her mouth from impressions left by life. She smiled with genuine concern, asking if I needed anything. She didn't know that her presence provided more than anything the doctors could prescribe. I wasn't blind or without a sense of smell to perceive the occasional alcohol or tobacco on her breath after she would go for a short drive each day. In the past, I would have felt insulted and been furious, but now I prayed for her to have the courage to escape any dependence that might control and destroy her life. I wanted nothing but the best for her. It wasn't about my reputation or the disappointment of a proud, dedicated parent, but the concern really was all about her, and I knew God would hear a prayer like that.

Over the next two weeks, I watched the "old Abby" that we had known continue to resurface. It was fairly easy for her to attend to my needs by bringing me an occasional cup of soup or tea and following me to and from the bathroom in case my broken foot needed to be coerced to keep pace with my other leg. Probably the most taxing time for both of us was when I changed clothes from nighttime pajamas to daytime sweat pants.

Bath times were challenging because of my injuries, literally from head to toe. The foot and ankle injury and incision in my groin made it difficult to maneuver clothing from the bottom half of my body while the trauma to my head and chest made it painful to remove or replace shirts. I had learned early that I could not move the left side of my chest, shoulder and arm because of the need to keep the leads from being disturbed in the chest cavity connecting the defibrillator cardiac device to my heart. I always wore a shirt that buttoned to allow my clothing to be removed without my having to lift my arm and shoulder.

Abby and Rick took on the task of helping me bathe. I had experienced enough sponge baths in the hospital to last me for quite a while, so even though taking the time to get into the bathtub or shower was a chore, it was worth it. Initially, Abby would help me step into the tub and steady me before and after I bathed. She sat on the side of the tub and helped me reach my back and wash my hair. It was a difficult and embarrassing time, literally exposing myself physically and emotionally before my daughter. I was weak, even frail, in my fragile and almost helpless condition. If she had wanted to take advantage of my pathetic state and limited abilities, it would have been her chance; but she didn't.

I was suddenly an adult dependent on my child, and that was an uncomfortable role reversal, although I felt completely loved, respected and cared for by her. She would carefully dry my back and legs, looking at the floor or into my face with eyes of compassion. I did not know at the time that just a month and a half from then, I would face another set of reversed roles when I walked into a residential nursing facility to find my own mother sitting in a wheelchair.

Trading Places

Six weeks after being released from the hospital, I perched myself near my mother's chair and wondered what had happened to my beautiful, strong, vibrant mom. She was confined, not because she was elderly, could not physically walk or wasn't mobile, but because as an Alzheimer's patient she had to be monitored and restrained from moving about without supervision. A portable alarm remained attached to her blouse as the attendants helped her into a twin-size bed, surrounded by rails and lined with disposable pads.

At dinnertime, I accompanied her to the dining room and asked her if she wanted her food. When she nodded I promptly spooned up a mouthful of cold baked beans and ground hamburger that I scraped from a stale bun. Carefully, I guided the spoonfuls into her mouth, trying not to drop or spill anything. After each bite, I patted the corners of her mouth to remove any trace of sauce or milk. I didn't want my mother to feel degraded by the help. I wanted her to know that it was a privilege for me to serve her as she had done for me countless times. I thought of how responsible I felt while performing this small task for my mom and how Abby must have felt helping me.

> *I found it very hard both to receive help from my daughter and to give help to my mother...*

I found it very hard both to receive help from my daughter and to give help to my mother, not because I didn't appreciate or accept the help, or want to serve my mother, but in both cases because that was "not the way it's supposed to be." My mother had always been the strong, independent woman in my family, and did not welcome assistance of any kind from anyone. I felt I was over-stepping my bounds, because if she had been cognizant of her surroundings, she would have felt humiliated. But the truth was, she didn't know that she was living in a nursing home at all, and most likely, wasn't aware of her family who wanted desperately to spend time with her.

In my situation, I had watched Abby care for the person who had always taken care of her, and we were both faced with the realization that everything and everyone changes. As people grow older, a change or switch in dominant roles tends to be one of the hardest changes in life. We want to continue to identify strength and security in the caregiver we have come to rely on and looked up to for answers, truth, and confidence. When that vision is shaken, we have to take a realistic look at that person and see them as mortal beings that we can identify with. Because I have been on the giving and receiving ends of this switch, I believe I can be more understanding and hopefully more compassionate toward both the caregiver and the one needing the help.

The truth is, I wish my mom could always be strong and talk with me about the tough times in life as well as enjoy sharing ideas about cooking, crafts and her knowledge about the farm and gardening. I wish, too, that my daughters could see me as independent and wise, and as a godly influence who has various shared interests in hobbies and in girl talk.

...time, circumstances and priorities play a huge role in the culmination of relationships.

Some of these things are still possible, the Lord willing, but time, circumstances and priorities play a huge role in the culmination of relationships. They may never be what they were or what we had wished for, but as long as there is life, there is hope. We have an opportunity to begin turning events into precious memories for generations to come. We can be grateful for memories, and as with everything else, not take for granted that ability to reminisce. Memories can emerge in either the development or commemoration stage, but both can be wonderful times. Sometimes we store those remembrances in shoe boxes or more elaborate albums and CDs, but whether they are shared around the dinner table with family, or savored privately on a handmade quilt in a sultry attic, they are invaluable and worthy of being treasured.

After more than a week after I had left the hospital, my insomnia peaked while I simultaneously became more aware of my physical limitations. Just when I thought my energy had returned, I noticed that I had dozed off during an afternoon TV show. I began opting to read and not just reading a good best-seller book, but actually reading and digging into the truths of God's Word, in a way I hadn't in a long time.

Of course, before my hospitalization, I had taken time for a 60-second devotional before each busy and important day, but suddenly, now I was reading books, chapters and passages that seemed to have been written just for me and to me. Every word, no matter where I read, jumped from the pages as a truth, suddenly applying to my circumstances and life. I had been an avid reader and had studied the Bible through various sources, commentaries and structured studies for many years after I had become a Christ follower in the 1980s. And when I was diagnosed with cardiomyopathy following the birth of April, I realized for the first time in my life that I had better get serious about some things, namely where I would spend eternity when my heart beats for the last time.

My spiritual life as a child had been mostly non-existent apart from the fact that when we purchased a farmhouse in the country from a local pastor, he must have believed that our family was ripe for the harvest, spiritually speaking. I'm sure after his initial efforts, he probably came to accept that the harvest may have been the more lofty goal, but that sowing a few seeds was the more attainable one. The soft-spoken preacher maintained ownership of the field across the road from our older frame house to provide grass for his cattle. He checked on the small herd every afternoon and often looked in on us to see if we were doing okay or needed anything. And as he would start to leave, he would always invite my mom to bring the family to church on Sunday. She would smile and promise that we would try to be there.

Sunday mornings became a war of the wills between my father and my mother. She began the day by finding out what he was planning that morning, and most of the time it included hunting with his father, repairing a dilapidated fence section or locating cattle or hogs MIA. If there were no pressing plans, she would sometimes ask if he would be interested in accepting the pastor's invitation to attend church services that week. It made it more difficult to refuse since the local country church was pastored by the man we had bought our farm and house from.

My sister and I sat on the edge of our full-size bed when we heard the discussion to see if we were going to be dressing in proper clothing for church or in worn jeans and t-shirts. Often we would hear what we perceived as positive talk and dress ourselves for the occasion only to be asked, "What are you doing with a dress on? We're not going anywhere. Church started five minutes ago." So, most of our church attendance consisted of religious holidays like Christmas and Easter. Occasionally we were told to get ready in short order and would arrive at the last minute, trying to find a seat without disrupting the small gathering but always managing to trip over someone's purse or sit on their Bible.

A woman placed her hand on my shoulder and whispered, "Don't you want to go too?"

The pastor continued to pursue us and invite us to services. Sometimes my mom felt an obligation to go after having made excuses week after week, and she would take my sister and me, often without my dad. It always seemed to be an emotional time for her when she went, especially during the time when the pastor gave an invitation to anyone who wanted to accept Christ as their Savior. The rest of the day she was usually more subdued than normal, although she didn't discuss these issues with me until I was older.

I remember a Sunday when the church service was coming to an end and the pastor gave an altar call. Almost immediately, the aisle leading to the front of the church was filled with every young person in the church. They knelt, many of them tearful, at the carved wooden altar and bowed their heads. A woman placed her hand on my shoulder and whispered, "Don't you want to go too?" With a nudge in their direction, I stepped out into the aisle lined with students praying and crying.

I knelt and listened to the other prayers because I didn't

know what to say. At that point, most of the others were moving into the pews near the pulpit and I followed. The pastor announced that the entire youth group as well as several adults had been saved that morning and would be baptized that evening. People were shaking our hands and congratulating us on our decision. I noticed that my mom and aunt were in the group, so when we left for home our conversation centered around the baptismal service to be held that evening in the river. I was grateful for the warm, summer temperatures as my mom told me about my grand-parents being baptized in the winter when the ice had to be broken on the pool of water.

As we arrived that afternoon, the group of converts formed a line in front of the water. The girls wore dresses with large safety pins holding them together between their legs so the motion of the water didn't float them over their heads. Mine was a bright blue, flower-print, a-line dress made by my mother, typical baptismal attire for that era and location. During our baptism, we held a white handkerchief over our noses before we were immersed and were baptized in the name of the Father, and the Son and of the Holy Ghost. Those who had already been saved stood on the bank of the river adjacent to those being baptized and sang "Shall We Gather at the River?" to welcome the newly saved Christians who had crossed over to that side. At the time I didn't understand the symbolism of the opposing sides, but honestly being so inexperienced with church life, I was just trying to follow the crowd and do what was expected.

My mom and I had a talk that night before bed and she

asked me how I felt now and I just said, "Fine, I guess." I knew something had changed inside and there was a different feeling about life than I had before, but my home life and school influences didn't foster that changed life. As time passed and I began junior high, I saw that the "in crowd" did not consist of the kids who were into church. I saw discrepancies in those who said they went to church, whether students, teachers or neighbors. I listened to my family talk about "church people" as though they were another race or from a foreign country even though they had lived in the same town with us for years. My mother and grandmother referred to church members and regular attenders as thinking they were better than us, and unfortunately they really believed that. With the pull of the world and no real commitment from my friends or role models, it was difficult for me to grasp the true meaning of Christianity.

...the prospect of a heart transplant or death did not allow time to ignore eternal possibilities...

Now, 23 years later, I wondered what that time had been about or if it had meant anything at all. Hearing from the doctors that my heart, damaged by an improperly placed epidural, could go into heart failure, the prospect of a heart transplant or death did not allow time to ignore eternal possibilities, which I understood from my limited knowledge of heaven and hell. Thankfully, the Bible makes certain areas very clear and simple, and I needed some straight answers. I had that limited knowledge because I had attended church off and on since age 9, but I also had a desire to know more.

When I married my husband, and by the time our daughters Abby and April were born, we attended church regularly. As a couple, we committed ourselves to raising our children in church and were there every time the doors were open. I had attended Bible studies weekly and continued seeking, reading and praying, but always struggled with being certain of my eternal destination and how to live the Christian life with assurance and confidence. I have jokingly said that I had walked the aisle more times than a peanut vendor at a ball game, but that was true! Every time our church invited a guest speaker or a revival was held featuring someone asking if we were sure if we died tonight, we would go to heaven, I was one of the first ones out of the pew to walk forward and give my life to Christ (again).

I felt I needed a once-and-for-all commitment that would seal my destiny.

I felt I needed a once-and-for-all commitment that would seal my destiny. I had heard a speaker on a local Christian radio station talk about how some people need to have a date that they can call into remembrance when doubt creeps in. Or, if you are not certain that there was a genuine repentance and commitment to the Lord, just remember that He knows your heart, and He gave His only Son so you could not only receive the gift of eternal life, but so you could settle that question once and for all. It does not require eloquent speech or a flood of tears to receive the gift of salvation, and doing so does not always result in an emotional response. But, if you need a date and time to feel secure in your decision as a Christ follower, then by all means, seek that peace. If not, you will be like the double-minded person in James 1:6-8, which reads, *"But when he asks, he must believe and not doubt, because he who doubts is like a wave of the sea, blown and tossed by the wind. That man should not think he will receive anything from the Lord; he is a double-minded man, unstable in all he does."*

Honestly, I was nauseous from the sea-sickness caused by waves of doubt. I decided to call our pastor's wife, who was a sweet lady and very genuine, about her walk with Christ. I had heard her speak once at a women's luncheon and trusted her guidance. When I began to lead into the conversation, it was as if she knew what I really wanted to talk about, and began telling me her story of struggling with questions about feeling secure in her faith in Christ. I was relieved and surprised as I listened to her recall the frustration of not knowing if she would spend eternity in heaven when she died. She told me that she, too, had experienced a medical scare when she was younger and was given a diagnosis of brain cancer. We talked for some time and she suggested that I call a young man who was dating her daughter and attending seminary. I agreed to contact him since I was familiar with him and his family, who also attended our church.

Wondering if he wanted to practice his theological training on me, I called him, unsure what the conversation might entail. The man was friendly and open as we began to talk about spiritual matters. He shared his own struggles, even as a seminary student, and having been raised in church. I heard these two committed, vibrant Christians readily tell me about their doubts, fears and frustrations in searching for truth and security in their faith and realized I wasn't the only one.

Following that day, I have never had a time of doubt about my eternal destination.

The following week, I walked the church aisle once more, this time not prompted by coercion or emotion, but by my own determination to settle that question for myself once and for all. I had been attending the church, but calmly stated that I wanted to give my life to Christ, and I did.

Following that day, I have never had a time of doubt about my eternal destination. Of course, I have had bouts of frustration, spiritual growth spurts and questions without answers about life issues and circumstances. But, as I continue reading the same Bible, many years later, it is still fascinating, intriguing, exciting and enlightening. At this crossroads in my life, I'm no longer looking for the answers to eternal security this time. I am, however, reminded that God cared enough to settle that concern, that He has more answers than I have questions, and that nothing is too hard for Him.

PART THREE

Love is a friendship that has caught fire. It is quiet understanding, mutual confidence, sharing and forgiving. It is a loyalty through good and bad. It settles for less than perfection and makes allowances for human weaknesses.

Love is content with the present, it hopes for the future and it doesn't brood over the past. It's the day-in and day-out chronicle of irritations, problems, compromises, small disappointments, big victories and working toward common goals.

If you have love in your life, it can make up for a great many things you lack. If you don't have it, no matter what else there is, it's not enough.

–Ann Landers, syndicated columnist
original source unknown

One Day At A Time

I rarely heard my mother sing. But as she stood in the kitchen preparing breakfast, I was at times aware of the sound of her voice singing slightly off key with the radio. More often, the song she seemed to identify with was one that was more of a personal prayer for her than a hit single.

> I'm only human, I'm just a woman
> Help me believe in what I could be
> And all that I am
> Show me the stairway, I have to climb
> Lord for my sake, teach me to take
> One day at a time

I don't remember my mom ever praying aloud with me and she would have been too embarrassed to pray in public, but occasionally I would pause in the hallway leading from my bedroom and listen as she voiced her heart's plea,

> "One day at a time sweet Jesus
>   That's all I'm asking from you
> Just give me the strength
>   To do everyday what I have to do
> Yesterdays gone sweet Jesus
>   And tomorrow may never be mine
> Lord help me today, show me the way
>   One day at a time"

–Christy Lane, *One Day at a Time*

My life has been driven by the anticipation of days and years yet to come in the future. Often I would lie awake at night contemplating how to react or defy a projected incident, only to awake to a day totally different from my prophetic scenario only a few hours before. I am regularly reminded that I do not have the promise of another day, another minute or even another breath.

As I walked through the days following my hospitalization, I also resisted my normal reaction – if I can't fix it, I must get on with life as if it never happened. I am quickly reminded in real ways that I wear the scars on my body and memories in my mind that refuse to allow me to forget.

Instead, I'm learning to choose to see life as a new gift everyday while using the experience and past to help others. I still get frustrated, anxious, worried and impatient but thankfully not as often and with a different perspective. Each day I intentionally focus on my present situation, not allowing my mind and thoughts to wander into the future and chase rabbits into dark holes. I remind myself regularly that the future is not mine and perhaps never will be. Thinking too far ahead could expose me to temptation and cause me to anticipate events and attitudes that God may never intend for me.

If my mind embraces future thoughts, I am confident that if those things would come to pass, He will give me the strength and help to either escape or handle it. There is no reason to try to meet difficult situations prematurely when I don't have the necessary strength or knowledge.

In other words, I'm learning to take *one day at a time*.

> I heard a story about a man who went to the pet store in search of a singing parakeet. Seems he was a bachelor and his house was too quiet. The store owner had just the bird for him, so the man bought it. The next day the bachelor came home from work to a house full of music. He went to the cage to feed the bird and noticed for the first time that the parakeet had only one leg. He felt cheated that he had been sold a one-legged bird, so he called and complained. "What do you want," the store owner responded, "a bird who can sing or a bird who can dance?" Disappointment is cured by revamped expectations.
> –Max Lucado, *Grace for the Moment, page 368*

My husband is not perfect. I've known that for some time,

but I have now come to realize many things in new ways. The truth is, over the past 28 years of marriage, I've become increasingly aware of his inadequacies, as well as my own. Many times, he does not meet my needs or expectations. He does not perform tasks and achieve accomplishments as quickly as I would like. Often, he hurts my feelings or seems insensitive, most of the time, without his knowledge. He doesn't play or watch sports, hunt, fish, play golf or even a musical instrument. He does not have a sense of adventure or "wild" nature and always plays things safe. My husband also has no desire for the pursuit of money, power or prestige.

The man actually enjoys menial tasks, including house-work (or so it would seem). If my grandmother were still alive, he would rival her in her ability to dust and wax hardwood floors as well as hand wash and dry dishes. He gets an uncanny sense of accomplishment from filling an entire sink full of scalding hot dishwater and producing squeaky clean plates and glasses and shiny kitchen countertops (yes, we do have a dishwasher).

And, at the end of the day, which is no later than 9 o'clock following his cup of coffee and bowl of chocolate ice cream, no matter what the day has held, he is able to lay his head on the pillow at night and fall into a deep slumber without hesitation (even while I'm trying to remind him of our many trials and tribulations). Many times, I don't think his head has fully made an impression on the pillowcase before the heavy sound of his lungs forcing air through his nostrils fills the bedroom.

But just as in the story about the parrot, my husband

provides exactly what I need. Did I mention that he is the kindest, gentlest man I have even met? I first met him when the two of us began working for a St. Louis Newspaper. He was a graphic artist and I was a reporter/writer. He drew the pictures to accompany the writers' stories. He had big, brown, kind eyes and always spoke shyly and softly to everyone. Since our marriage, he has come alongside me with encouraging words and actions that show that I can trust him and count on him to be by my side (to the end).

While I was in the neuro-trauma intensive care unit at the hospital, he rarely left my side. He slept in a hard hospital chair next to my hospital bed and attentively fed and cared for me day and night for 12 days while I was in the hospital and continued doing so after we came home. Some days, I remember him placing ice chips on my tongue to cool the fever, and softening my cracked dry lips with a soothing balm. I know he was exhausted but he never complained.

He is not boastful or prideful, although he possesses amazing talents and abilities in art and architectural design. He is respectful and protective of me, our daughters, and our granddaughter. He is a gentleman; he still opens my car door and waits for me to walk in front of him or by his side when we go out. My husband has the attributes of a meek man, which are sometimes mistaken for weakness.

I have heard it said that "meekness is not weakness, but it is power under control." The analogy given was that of a stallion who was of great value to his trainer when he was disciplined to the point of controlling his natural tendencies to exercise his rebellious nature. Although he could have rebelled against his trainer and remained a beautiful steed in the wild, he chose to become obedient, groomed and trained to be an exceptional animal. A man who chooses self-control over selfishness and invites the Lord to mold him as the potter fashions the clay is one who not only loves his family but glorifies His God.

It was an amazing moment when I stopped choosing to look at my husband's faults and inabilities and chose to appreciate the fact that he unquestionably loves God and his family above all else, including himself or selfish gain. No, he can't dance (or sing), but he is exactly the man God has for me to spend this life with and share this amazing ride called life.

My daughters are the apples of my eye. They are intelligent, sensitive, generous, beautiful young women. Our relationships have been extremely close and are the twin joys of my life. When they were babies, I couldn't stop looking at them. They amazed me even as I considered the intricacies of a tiny helpless fetus developing into a viable yet delicate baby, unfinished and yet so perfect. I was in my late 20s when I gave birth to Abby and early 30s when April was born and lost two subsequent pregnancies.

When each of the girls was born, I treasured them, and frankly, my world revolved around them. I made them the determining factor in any and all decisions, and placed them ahead of all relationships or priorities. I know as moms, we are all in love with our babies, so I'm not talking about giving proper care and attention to or enjoying your child. My priorities, to put it bluntly, were unhealthy, but my motives at the time were pure. I simply wanted to make sure they felt loved and valued.

I had experienced a difficult childhood from birth and wanted my own children's lives to be free from feelings of rejection and abandonment. Growing up, my daughters never wondered if they were loved. I'm happy that they can know that truth. As young adults, they have independently made choices in life that have brought joy and heartache, as we all have. But the truth is, I have only been disappointed when I focus on my own expectations. I spent many years envisioning fearless missionaries to China, crusaders for evangelical freedoms. Or at least they would become super home-schooling moms with pastors or full-time ministry husbands and a house full of adoring children – none of which at this point has come to fruition. They are still very young, and I know God can use them in any way He chooses, and that His plans are much higher than mine.

Like a hen gathering her chicks under her wing, I protected and sheltered them from the falling sky.

I wanted smooth sailing for them, but ripples and storms have proven to require difficult maneuvering in some areas. Like a hen gathering her chicks under her wing, I protected and sheltered them from the falling sky. But as I see them look up, I know they are beginning to realize that the One who has saved them will keep them. As always, I cherish the time I spend with them, sometimes comparing myself with them when I was their ages. I realize quickly where they are and how mature they are compared to me. Suddenly, my hope, appreciation and gratitude are restored.

My relationship with my daughters has matured and changed as they have grown up and learned to take responsibility. The two of them continue to overcome trials and obstacles in life, many times in different ways than I have. I'm sure they will continue to endure and grow in the future. But, more than anything, I hold on to a certainty that they are loved, not only by their father and me, and other family members and friends, but that they are loved and cherished by God, and that we will someday spend eternity in Heaven together. Life as we know it on this earth and as we know and relate to one another, will be so much better and deeper.

Only be careful, and watch yourselves closely so that you do not forget the things your eyes have seen or let them slip from your heart as long as you live. Teach them to your children and to their children after them. Deuteronomy 4:9

THE QUESTION "WHY?"

When I was a child, I spoke and thought and reasoned as a child. But when I grew up, I put away childish things. 1 Corinthians 13:11 (NLT)

I sometimes wonder what the collapse, cardiac arrest, hospitalization and recovery time were all about. Believe me, I have asked the "why" question, but not in the way you might think. I instead ask why He chose to save me from death and allow me the privilege of another day of life, especially a second time. I still don't have the answer and I'm not arguing or spending a lot of time looking for it. I think when something life-changing happens that gets our attention, and we have learned something from the time or trial, it was a fruitful experience. I have had the opportunity to tell countless people of God's goodness and mercy to me, although I find it easier to slip back into complaining about the aches, pains and limitations than praising God in all things.

During my healing, and after the get-well cards and delivered home cooked meals had ceased, I wanted to have a grateful, joyful heart. Just as I anticipate another page of a long-awaited best-selling book so I can read the next twist and turn in the story, I look forward to the next page in life with its unknowns. It's an exciting time as the unknown unfolds and becomes reality. Just as the cardiac arrest certainly was not an expected detour for my family and me, God promises that *"in all things God works for the good of those who love him, who have been called according to his purpose."* Romans 8:28

How that plays out is not something we always understand or would choose, but faith is often illuminated during these times, and we find strength by relying on Him. Honestly, I don't think I would ever choose weakness over my own strength and ability, even though the Bible tells us of God's power and provision, or as Paul put it, *"For when I am weak, then I am strong."* That is a hard truth for me to grasp and practice. I grew up in a family where weakness was a definite negative and relying on others was thought of as frailty, laziness and a chink in your armor. My mom used to say that she would walk across the street to find out the time before she would ask someone standing next to her on the street corner. I often wondered why she would hesitate to ask a person, especially someone she knew, living in our small, friendly town where everyone knew everyone. But, I believe that my mom was anxious around some people for fear of being judged or criticized.

In her earlier stages of Alzheimer's, she was often confused about a person's intentions if she was in a public setting. Once when she went to the beauty salon, she became upset because she thought the women were all talking and whispering about her. She was convinced that they were yelling profanities at her while she sat in the chair. The salon owner and stylist were familiar with my mom and the other customers who were there but never heard anyone say anything out of line.

A similar incident occurred at a church service in which she thought the women were whispering defamatory, derogatory comments as she walked into the building. The disease has a devastating affect on the mind and personality, but I know Mom always had a hard time trusting people, even though she loved being with others and always enjoyed her many friends. As a kindergarten teacher/aide, she taught generations of children who adored her.

I longed for her to open her beautiful blue eyes and know who I was.

Recently, I visited my mom in the nursing home to which she had been transferred after an illness and brief hospitalization. The facility was holding a Christmas program for the residents and after the Santa impersonation and singing, one of the workers came to her room to ask if she had opened the gift that sat next to her bed. I explained that I had been sitting with her for five hours, but she was still not awake. The nurse on duty had informed me that my mom had stayed awake all night and didn't go to bed until 10:30 that morning. I knew she was tired and sleepy and needed her rest, but I longed for her to open her beautiful blue eyes and know who I was. The kind worker sat on the edge of her bed and tried to wake her by speaking softly to her, but to no avail.

She bent down and picked up the bag decorated with glitter and snowflakes, pulling the gift from the bright red tissue paper. It was a stuffed dog with big buttons, zippers, snaps, and shoelaces. As she removed the animal from its box, she told me, "Mrs. Henson was my teacher in kindergarten and she also taught and cared for my son." She explained that each year the nursing staff bought individual gifts for the patients and she chose my mom because she was her favorite teacher. Giving the soft, felt, tan and orange dog a tug on his ear, the young woman turned the animal over to reveal the inscription, "To: Mrs. Henson, Merry Christmas. Love, Ashley."

She handed the gift to me and wiped a tear from her eye as she got up to leave. "This was her favorite thing to do with the kids. She taught us how to zip our coats and tie our shoes using a stuffed dog like this one when I was a kid in her classroom. She was a great teacher. Everyone loved her at school and they still do here because she is such a wonderful lady."

Often we see our parent as our caregiver, cook, nurse, and so on, but fail to realize how they have touched other people's lives. The visit to the nursing home was a mixed blessing as I saw how disease and time can ravage the body and the brain, but it also helped me remember that spending your life investing in others often pays dividends to not only the one who sacrificed but also those who love that person. I'm sure that it is often many years after a parent has given sacrificially of themselves to their children that they are appreciated, but hopefully they will have known that feeling of value and esteem before it is too late.

Life is short and it should be lived NOW! I don't mean at the expense of tossing out common sense or planning for the future, but enjoying every day as a gift from God. Much of youth is wasted, but we don't realize that until we are looking in the rearview mirror.

Life cannot be lived through other people. I lived a lot of

my life struggling to please someone, or trying to live up to another's expectations. For many years I tried to become a person that I thought others would admire or at least respect because of my sacrifice. The problem is that the good deed is done for the wrong reason and motivation if you are trying to get others' approval. You miss the blessing and the lesson. I am beginning to understand that life lessons are like gold coins. If we collect them along the way and invest wisely, we will continue to be richer in life and give to others from our overflow of abundance.

> *Trust in the LORD with all your heart and lean not on your own understanding; in all your ways acknowledge him, and he will make your paths straight.* Proverbs 3:5-6

> *Think over what I say, for the Lord will give you understanding in everything.* 2 Timothy 2:7 (ESV)

> *Who is wise and understanding among you? By his good conduct let him show his works in the meekness of wisdom.* James 3:13 (ESV)

> *Keep them and do them, for that will be your wisdom and your understanding in the sight of the peoples, who, when they hear all these statutes, will say, "Surely this great nation is a wise and understanding people."* Deuteronomy 4:6 (ESV)

Get wisdom; get insight; do not forget, and do not turn away from the words of my mouth.

Proverbs 4:5 (ESV)

WHAT HAVE YOU
LEARNED, DOROTHY?

I remember that question running through my mind and wondering what one of the wisest women in film history might have said to me. At a pivotal point in the movie, "The Wizard of Oz," Dorothy is left behind by the great and powerful Wizard himself because he "doesn't know how it works," referencing "it" being the hot air balloon after its spoiled launch, as he floats off in a solo flight to Kansas. Heartbroken because she misses Aunt Em and Uncle Henry, Dorothy begins to cry with her cohorts near her (as if a scarecrow, tin man, and cowardly lion were any real consolation). Suddenly, a large soap bubble appears containing none other than the wisest woman in all of Oz. Dorothy expresses her grief and frustration as Glinda, good witch of the North, simply says, "You've always had the power to go back to Kansas," explaining to Dorothy's friends, "but she wouldn't have believed me. She had to learn it for herself."

The Tin Man simply asks, "What have you learned, Dorothy?" "Well," she begins, "I think that it wasn't enough just to want to see Uncle Henry and Aunt Em – and it's that, if I ever go looking for my heart's desire again, I won't look any further than my own backyard. Because if it isn't there, I never really lost it to begin with! Is that right?"

"That's all it is!" Glinda replies, confirming the girl's revelation, and Dorothy is transported via ruby slippers through time and space to her cozy bed in Kansas, surrounded by her family and friends. So, I have slipped on my red fuzzy house slippers and asked myself, "Dorothy, what have you learned?"

Because I usually think with a pen in my hand, I began to write down the thoughts that came to mind as I pondered God's truths. I am primarily a visual learner and a "list" person, so I asked God to show me things in my life that I have learned through this life experience and other events for my personal growth and to help others. Not only things I "have learned" in reference to the past, whether last week or last year, but also what I am in the process of learning "today."

Not only have I learned the lessons, but I am understanding and applying the truths behind those lessons. Having numbered my yellow legal pad from one to five, I filled those slots and quickly added subsequent numbers. The lessons, of course, are endless, but God knows He can only feed me spoonfuls at a time. But each bite was nourishment for my soul.

LACK OF TRUST

The first lesson for me sounded simple, but if I were honest, it is an ongoing struggle. Many times I've heard well-meaning Christians say, "Just trust God." It has been difficult for me to admit that trust and reliance on a loving God who wants to do good to me and for me without expecting anything in return are hard to embrace. I know when I'm not trusting, because in those moments I trade the calm, peaceful, confidence of trust for worry and anxiety. It's my nature to problem solve and that has worked well in circumstances at work and home where problems have logical solutions, and where I can help myself and others move past a difficulty. But when I can't solve or resolve something, in creeps anxiety and unnecessary burdens. Anxiety is the absence of trust and I know it well. We are instructed,

"Don't fret or worry. Instead of worrying, pray. Let petitions and praises shape your worries into prayers, letting God know your concerns. Before you know it, a sense of God's wholeness, everything coming together for good, will come and settle you down. It's wonderful what happens when Christ displaces worry at the center of your life."

Philippians 4:6-7 (MSG)

We often act as though knowing in advance about an incident or life change will help prepare us and better equip us to handle the trial. Wouldn't it be strange if we came into this life knowing all the key circumstances and events before they occurred? They could be included with a manual for parents, outlining the baby's life through infancy, youth, adulthood and old age. For instance, if we knew a tragic accident was going to happen we would prepare for it in advance or, better yet, try to avoid or prevent it from happening. But changing that event would set the course for another. The truth is, we don't live in a protective bubble, but we do trust in a God who promises, *"I will never leave you nor forsake you."* Joshua 1:5

In reality, would knowing life's events in advance really bring us peace and happiness? Even with my need to control and eliminate undue surprises, I have to say I am glad that God has protected me from worrying and trying to manipulate circumstances that were out of my ability to do anything about. I worry far too much as it is, such that I identify with Mark Twain, who once said, " I have suffered a great many tragedies in my life, most of which never came to pass."

Trust God.

> *Surely God is my salvation; I will trust and not be afraid.* Isaiah 12:2a

As a very young child I experienced feelings of rejection and abandonment that have affected relationships throughout my life. My mother was divorced and a single mom by the age of 20, following an abusive marriage, so I spent my early childhood years living with grandparents and relatives while she worked to support us. Often I stayed with any available babysitter – too many to count and too many unqualified to care for a child.

Even as I grew older, I still experienced those fears and questioned the motives of those I interacted with. However, as young children, we naturally want to trust our parents and peers. Even when things are not right or we are used or taken advantage of, we expect the best from those around us and believe they will guard and protect us. It is only as we get older and begin to question motives and actions over a period of time that we begin to guard ourselves against others.

This unhealthy suspicion of others spills into our relationship with God. Distrust can eventually destroy our relationships with people and God when it becomes our shield. We all have disappointments and betrayals in our lives. What we do with those will either embitter us and prevent us from seeking an intimate, vulnerable closeness with others or cause us to look at their faults and frailties and love them despite their imperfections. Seeing their humanity and allowing it to build the relationship, using the differences to bond rather than destroy, is always the goal.

Even harder for me to realize is the fact that not only is it okay to ask for God's help, but that He desires and expects us to rely on Him. He uses that trust and reliance to show his faithfulness. Those building blocks of hope strengthen us so we continue to tell others of His faithfulness and our trust.

Yet the Lord longs to be gracious to you.
Isaiah 30:18

God actually looks forward to hearing his children ask for His help, and our asking deepens our relationship. I know when my daughters or my granddaughter call for me and ask for my help, I am excited about the opportunity to do something for them. It's not a chore or imposition, but a privilege, knowing that we have a relationship that allows them to feel comfortable enough to ask me for my help. If we can't trust Him, we will find it impossible to worship; if we don't worship, trust and obey Him, He is not our God.

My soul finds rest in God alone. **Trust in him at all times**, *O people; pour out your hearts to him, for God is our refuge.*

Psalm 62:1a, 8 (emphasis mine)

*May the God of hope fill you with all joy and peace as you **trust in him**, so that you may overflow with hope by the power of the Holy Spirit.*

Romans 15:13 (emphasis mine)

WHY FORGIVE?

I never considered myself an unforgiving person, but after my accident, I began thinking about the people who had visited me in the hospital and at home, or sent cards. As I looked at the names written in their personal handwriting, I thought of the time they must have put into choosing a card, writing a get well wish, addressing and sending it in the mail. Many were relatives, co-workers and friends I had met through various associations. At times, I was surprised to see a name, recalling a difference of opinion or perceived mutual distancing. I found it hard to believe that my mind could turn initially to a negative conversation or incident, even after knowing this person was praying for me, as they said in the card, and wishing me well. God showed me that those attitudes are not only harmful, but sinful. We even pray, *"Forgive us our debts, as we also have forgiven our debtors."* Matthew 6:12

One day when I woke up extremely early, I was exhausted and agitated about the continuing pain from the surgery. I was mad at the world, and when I couldn't get my shoulder to cooperate or listen, I began to take out my fatigue-induced annoyance on my husband. Since he and the dog were the only ones around, I figured I had known my husband longer and he was bigger, so I'd begin with him and move down the food chain. I couldn't think of anything good about that man, even though I knew he had been by my side and cared for me without fail for months, actually years. I managed to probe my memory for anything I could find that was a negative trait. It's amazing how you can turn even positive traits to negatives when you're trying. On that occasion my neurosurgeon would have been proud of the recall abilities of my frontal lobe.

That night, I slept even worse. Everything about my body ached. I awoke even earlier the next morning, and as those who know me can attest, that is not a natural phenomenon for me. I have insisted that God never intended for me to see a sunrise; that's why there are sunsets. Besides, if he had wanted me to see a sunrise, he would have scheduled it for later in the day.

I am, by nature, a night person, so the fact that it was still dark outside and my husband was still in bed were two red flags for me without even having to look at the alarm clock. (I'm sure you have guessed that my husband is an early morning person. He wakes up naturally at 4:30 a.m. to begin his routine, even though he works from home and could sleep until noon if he wanted to.)

I decided to read my Bible that morning to ask God to help me with the pain. After using a Max Lucado daily devotional, I quickly moved to an Oswald Chambers reading, then wisdom from Charles Stanley. I couldn't understand why all the readings for the day seemed to deal with forgiveness rather than healing. I was in pain, and forgiving or not forgiving my husband or anyone else wasn't going to help with the real problem.

Closing the books, I sat with my head in my hands, asking for God's help. I was miserable and at the end of my rope. Closing my eyes and taking a deep breath, I realized the morning sun was beginning to peek over the top of the curtain. His words came to my heart and mind: *"Because of the Lord's great love we are not consumed, for his compassions never fail. They are new every morning; great is your faithfulness."* Lamentations 3:22-23

But, why do I need them "every" morning? He quickly and lovingly spoke to my heart, "Because you need a fresh start every day. You sin every day. Whether in blatant disobedience and awareness or in unconscious blindness and ignorance, you sin." Then, the devotional readings came flooding back to my mind. Clearly, I am often easily offended. From experience, I know that childhood hurts can manifest themselves in the perception of an insult or attack, leading to resentment and an unforgiving spirit. Even when you aren't aware of those thoughts, they often become obvious in relationships, in ways unrelated to the original offense.

And the peace of God, which transcends all understanding, will guard your hearts and your minds in Christ Jesus. Philippians 4:7

I once read, "Resentment is like drinking poison and waiting for the other person to die." In other words, unforgiveness is not only detrimental to our health, emotional well-being and relationships, it will destroy your life, robbing you of the joy and intimacy God wants you to have with Him and others who bless you. Suppressing or denying a feeling of offense is not healthy either. Your feelings are real, but dealing with those feelings in a healthy way produces joy and forgiveness in place of repressed anger for another day and another person.

Many times a person isn't aware he or she has offended us, and often a misunderstanding can be resolved with less effort than fuming and rehearsing the conversation in our mind. Whether the hurt was intentional or in ignorance, it is our responsibility to protect our minds and most importantly our relationship with God. Admit your hurts and feelings, asking for His help. A pity party is often poorly attended, and even if guests come, they rarely bring snacks; so do yourself a favor and deal with unforgiveness by admitting you can't do without His help.

> *In your anger do not sin. Do not let the sun go down while you are still angry, and do not give the devil a foothold.* Ephesians 4:26-27

A LITTLE R-E-S-P-E-C-T

Often we learn lessons that resurface later in life. Our experiences not only shape us immediately, but many times have a lasting effect in helping us determine our attitudes toward people and God. Valuing and showing respect for human life has always been modeled for me by my parents and grandparents. Because my mom worked in the Head Start public school program, she would often speak about the children who would come into her class every day without coats in the winter or having eaten only the food available at the cafeteria at school once a day. Some lacked good hygiene and wore the same dirty clothes for weeks at a time. If we had anything negative to say about their appearance or mannerisms, my mom would immediately set us straight and remind us not to "get above our raisin'." She made it clear that she had better not hear us acting as though we were superior to any person.

We certainly didn't have anything to brag about or any basis on which to consider our lifestyle as placing us in an elevated class. In fact, as I look back, we were a common, blue-collar family that lived on a small farm while my father was employed as a factory worker at Brown Shoe Company during the day and loaded sacks onto trucks at the feed store at night.

My mom dropped out of school at age 17, but went back and completed her GED while I was in high school. She was hired at the local elementary school as a teacher's aide and took several college classes in the evenings. We lived within our means, eating what the vegetable garden, fruit trees and livestock provided. My mom made many of our clothes on her sewing machine, and I never owned a prom dress or went to the beauty salon. My cousin let me borrow one of her dresses from a previous year when I was nominated for FHA (Future Homemakers of America) Queen and a dress was required for the school yearbook. I never seemed to realize that we were poor because I loved my family, and as a child, you often surround yourself with those who have a similar standard of living. Having a pride issue because of affluence or culture wasn't a problem. Living in a depressed, lower socio-economic area surrounded us with many families who struggled financially and had far less than we did.

Our humble circumstances worked the same way in encouraging us to respect life in all forms: infancy, youth, old age and death. One summer while attending college, I found myself needing a job between semesters, so I applied at the funeral home in my rural hometown, which was hiring a receptionist. The owners had met and married when they were teenagers and had quickly begun working in their family's small but lucrative business. As a young girl in my early 20s, I wasn't sure how I would react to the creepy, scary place that prepared dead bodies for burial.

I was, of course, familiar with the funeral home and its owners because it was the only establishment in the area where I had attended the funerals of family or townspeople who had died. However, I felt that I knew them on a deeper level because of an observation that had made an impression on me. The local drug store where I had worked a few years earlier as a teenager at the soda fountain often brought townspeople for a quick lunch and conversation. On many occasions I had heard customers nervously try to joke with the funeral director, who would come through the doors at lunch time for a grilled sandwich or an early afternoon soda. Those who didn't know the somber well-dressed businessman very well would sometimes say, "Hey, how's business? I hear people are just dying to get into your place." Or, "Hey Marvin, I hear the funeral home business is really dead around here lately." Some would laugh, others would nervously chuckle, fumbling with their grilled cheese sandwiches or playing with the crushed ice in their Coke glasses with their straws.

Looking up briefly at one another seated in the long row of red vinyl-topped chrome bar stools, more often than not, the people would grow quiet. Patrons peered downward, hoping the idiot who started the joke would stop before someone in the drugstore was hurt by the reminder that they had lost a loved one, regardless of whether the loss was current or the jokes opened hurtful memories. The funeral director always remained expressionless, and made it known on several occasions that death is a serious issue and is never to be taken lightly, and that the deceased must always be treated with dignity and respect. I was 15 then, and that resolve and respect made an impression on me. When I worked for the business later, I learned that attitude never changed; it was the same standard behind closed doors as I had seen in public. Life is to be cherished and respected at all stages.

STAY POSITIVE

The precepts of the LORD are right, giving joy to the heart.   Psalm 19:8

I know that many people have had experiences involving catastrophic illnesses and even near-death incidents. Others who have not experienced such events personally have shared a life-shattering occurrence with a close friend or family member. When such an event happens, life is changed forever, regardless of the outcome. In my case, my physical limitations brought with them permanent and short-term consequences, my mental ability was hindered temporarily, and my position at work and my lifestyle were challenged and altered.

However, something I noticed as an immediate positive result was that those people who had been close to me not only continued the relationship, but increased their level of commitment and intimacy. Those who had been near me when I had initially experienced the cardiac arrest were the most shaken, and the event seemed to have a real impact on their perspectives on life. I imagine many of them became much nicer to everyone, from their spouses, children and neighbors to the local grocery store checker. Seeing death on the face of someone you know has a powerful affect, even if you aren't extremely close to them.

I often wonder what kind of perspective emergency medical personnel have on life and death. While recovering at home after being released from the hospital, I would periodically stop in at the office where I worked to see staff members and volunteers. I had served as a volunteer for several years and had been hired onto staff two years earlier, so my involvement had been extensive. I missed seeing everyone as well as the schedule and routine of my job. It was a nice feeling to be missed, appreciated and cared for by so many people. But especially during the first visit to the office building, it was hard to keep haunting visions of the incident from flooding my mind. As soon as I stepped off the elevator, co-workers flocked to my side in anticipation and with questions about my recovery and health.

I quickly noticed that the staff members who had witnessed or been within view of the incident were more quiet and subdued. The last time they had seen me was when they watched as my lifeless body lay on the floor. My current state of health was a definite improvement, but I could see that the lingering reminders haunted them. Each time I visited, one co-worker in particular would burst into tears or avoid eye contact as she hurried to her office. I'm still not certain if she was frightened by the physical image of me with a black eye and shaved head or if I was a reminder of her own mortality and brevity of life. Everyone involved with the incident was affected, but each in his or her own way, depending on personal experiences and relationships.

Having a positive attitude and sense of humor can go a long way in any recovery after a crisis or trauma. When I came to the place where I felt that I could cut the long hair from the right side of my head to match the shaved left side, it was a big day. I searched for hours on the internet to find a hairstyle that I could sport, but there were none short enough. So I searched for men's styles and they weren't short enough either!

So, I walked into the salon where I had gotten the last cut and style – which I had never had the chance to enjoy – and asked for the male stylist who had attended to me in the past. Given his own spiky, jet-black locks, I considered pointing to his hair and saying, "I want that haircut," but once again, it was too long. Since the stylist had heard about my accident from my daughter, he welcomed me with a hug and immediately went to work discussing the few available options. It was comforting to know that he had personal experience working with head trauma victims. His wife had been in a car accident several years earlier and her head had been shaved similarly to mine. He was compassionate and understanding, so after a while I relaxed and trusted him to do his best with what little he had to work with.

Within a short time (no pun intended) my 12 inches of hair was lying on the floor and I was laughing and having a great time. A chic, sassy lady emerged from the chair that I had dreaded. I could have cried or complained, which would have been a more natural response, but I decided to enjoy what hair I did have and enjoy the change. Who knows? I may never grow it long again.

Life often gives us opportunities, but when we look at change or a situation only as having taken or stolen something from us, we will never grow and embrace anything new. Enjoy life, laugh at yourself and with others, and constantly look to seek out the positive in every situation.

He will yet fill your mouth with laughter and your lips with shouts of joy.　　　　　　　　　Job 8:21

REALLY ENJOY LIFE

But may the righteous be glad and rejoice before
God; may they be happy and joyful.   Psalm 68:3

If joy is only in our control, we will lose
it when life-altering events occur.

After I began to think about the impact of my collapse and
what a life-changing event it had been, I had to ask myself
what I had learned about the frailty and brevity of life, and
what I would do with my remaining time. I couldn't just
return to life as if nothing significant had happened. Shortly
after being released from the hospital I remember riding
along with my husband to the grocery store but staying in
the car to wait for him.

As I watched shoppers go into and come out of the store,
I couldn't help but think how many of them likely thought
very little, if anything, about what they were doing. Had
life been routine for them? Were they in a hurry or looking
forward to spending an evening with friends or family for
dinner? If they knew that this was their last day on earth,
would they have done anything differently?

I remember seeing a movie once called "The Bucket
List," with Jack Nicholson and Morgan Freeman playing
two dying men who write out a list of things they want to
accomplish before they die. Even though the two hospital
roommates have their illnesses in common, they are worlds
apart in terms of their earthly achievements and relationships

in their 60-plus years of life.

These mature men begin to live out their dying wishes together, first by challenging life by jumping from an airplane and driving fast sports cars, and then by indulging in expensive dining and hotels. But after the rush of excitement is over and the cancer continues to plague their bodies, the two have to make definite decisions about the importance of their families, about how to handle regrets and accomplishments, but more importantly about what happens after death. Along with some purely comedic moments, some truthful scenes in the movie pointed out the importance of placing family over money and relationships above personal achievement.

The hard truth is that people are affected differently when they come face to face with the realization that life must end on this earth. I've talked to plenty of people, especially when they are young, strong, healthy and almost invincible, who think it is unimportant to reflect on this all-important gift that we so often take for granted. It is necessary to ask ourselves seriously, "Why am I here? Why has God chosen to allow me to be on this earth?" I know from personal experience that if He withholds even one breath, life cannot be sustained.

Reflecting on life issues should not produce a morbid, depressed, life-stealing view where you aren't making plans for the future or even buying green bananas; I'm talking about having an excitement about, and appreciation and gratitude for, the opportunity to enjoy life, love God and love people.

The thief comes only in order to steal and kill and destroy. I came that they may have and enjoy life, and have it in abundance (to the full, till it overflows). John 10:10 (AMPLIFIED)

If we truly believed that, we would live differently.

COUNT YOUR BLESSINGS

We can't see how we will get through the future
if we forget how we got through the past.

I challenge everyone I talk with about my incident and their personal trials to keep a thankfulness or gratitude journal for themselves as a reminder of the day's blessings. Doing so will also help you to intentionally look for things to write in your journal. I recommend starting with three entries each day, thinking about the happiness and goodness you have experienced in a 24-hour period.

There are days when those moments are hard to identify, which is all the more reason to determine to find a bright spot in a dark day. It doesn't need to be monumental or life-changing. As a matter of fact, it is better when we can enjoy a good meal with our family, find a great deal on a fun pair of shoes, or peer out the window to watch a bluebird enjoy a sunflower seed. There is something in every day to enjoy.

There are many dangers in losing your joy and gratitude. We often begin focusing on our rights, being served by others and consumed by the world. It always results in frustration, disappointment and discouragement. Some psychologists and university professors recommend journaling as a thera-peutic way of helping people manage and deal with negative thoughts. Maintaining a gratitude journal primarily causes your thoughts to be focused on the positives and helps you to pull yourself out of the mire of pessimism. I'm sure that's what Paul meant when he wrote,

"Summing it all up, friends, I'd say you'll do best by filling your minds and meditating on things true, noble, reputable, authentic, compelling, gracious—the best, not the worst; the beautiful, not the ugly; things to praise, not things to curse. Put into practice what you learned from me, what you heard and saw and realized. Do that, and God, who makes everything work together, will work you into his most excellent harmonies." Philippians 4:8-9 (MSG)

NO DOUBT

One of the enemy's most effective tools to rob us of our
joy and peace is to use doubt and discouragement.

It was a foggy Monday morning, and the sun struggled to illuminate the sky. It was 7 a.m. and the sun arrived just as scheduled, ready and willing to do its job. But something was hindering it from performing its duty, a purpose it was designed for from its creation. The interference was only temporary, however, and as I watched for the next hour, I saw that after a time the powerful rays burned away the misty haze to unveil a brilliant light and usher in the natural warmth to welcome the day. In all appearances, the sun was not going to prevail that morning. But slowly the fog was lifted. Nothing could stop God's will or His purpose.

The sun would shine, and the same is true in our lives. God has a plan and purpose for our lives, but we often allow a fog to settle over our minds and hearts, often inhibiting an answer or a breakthrough. What is clouding your thinking today? I know I struggled with being "double-minded" for many years. I knew that Jeremiah 29:11 said, *"'For I know the plans I have for you,' declares the Lord, 'plans to prosper you and not to harm you, plans to give you hope and a future.'"*

Those are powerful words, and I believed what they said, until…I began to think and reason and calculate and "doubt" what I had heard from God or whether I had heard correctly from Him. Enter my doubting, evil twin, questioning as

Eve did when she conversed with the serpent in the garden of Eden: *"Did God really say, 'You must not eat from any tree in the garden?' "* Genesis 3:1. The challenge of doubt crossed the threshold of Eve's mind and her ability to hold onto truth was compromised at that very moment. She even managed to tell the serpent what God had told her, almost as if to replay the command to convince and remind herself: *"The woman said to the serpent, 'We may eat fruit from the trees in the garden, but God did say, "You must not eat fruit from the tree that is in the middle of the garden, and you must not touch it, or you will die."'"* Genesis 3:2-3

But Satan challenged her weakness and confidence as well as God's authority. He quickly confronted her by questioning her belief initially, and immediately planting doubt to produce distrust and a double-minded spirit. Finally, he deliberately and blatantly removed God from the throne of Eve's mind, causing her to question her ability to discern truth and believe what God had revealed to her. With all the false authority the devil could muster, he proclaimed, *"You will not surely die."* (Genesis 3:4) We know that statement was a lie, and the decision to take the bait of Satan wasn't a smart move on Eve's part. She not only experienced death, but also set in motion the penalty for us all. In the first chapter of the New Testament book of James, the Bible is clear in directing us to God for answers, trusting Him to supply our needs and checking doubt at the prayer closet door:

"If any of you lacks wisdom, he should ask God, who gives generously to all without finding fault, and it will be given to him. But when he asks, he must believe and not doubt,

because he who doubts is like a wave of the sea, blown and tossed by the wind. That man should not think he will receive anything from the Lord; he is a double-minded man, unstable in all he does." James 1:5-8

An indecisive attitude generally points to a distrusting spirit. Many people who have had hurtful and tragic childhoods or unfaithful mates or spouses have a hard time trusting and therefore transfer that same cynicism to God. I had a trail of excuses for not trusting God because of past failed relationships, childhood abuse and feelings of rejection, but God continued to pursue me and show me how trustworthy He is and has been in my life as well as those of countless friends and family members.

VALUE ACHIEVEMENTS
(NO MATTER HOW SMALL)

Recently, my three-year-old granddaughter came running into my bathroom with a gleeful squeal: "I did it all by myself, Nana!" The reflection in the mirror told me that her pink and yellow polka dot shirt should have had a lower neckline in the front than the back. And, as I turned to applaud her achievement, I noticed her glittery Barbie tennis shoes were facing opposing feet, causing her to look like a penguin. Nonetheless, I quickly bent over to give her a hug and enthusiastic praise.

I was genuinely proud of her for working so hard to accomplish a task many three-year-olds could not have. (And besides, she is my only granddaughter, can do no wrong and is always adorable.) She did a cute little pirouette in the middle of the floor, which was not easy with shoes on the wrong feet, but lost her balance and fell into the shower door. She began to cry and I felt badly for her as she went from feelings of exuberance and pride to frustration and pain.

Life's like that a lot. We're up one minute, feeling good about what we've accomplished and how we've grown, and the next thing you know, we're thrown off balance by poor fitting shoes, a single quick turn, blindsided by a closed door, and down we go. Just when we thought everything was moving in the right direction and we had taken two steps forward, suddenly we are three steps behind. Most often, our pride is what is wounded the most, but sometimes it is hard to get back up and keep trying.

I recalled a few short months before when I could not feed

myself, speak clearly, write legibly or perform simple hygiene tasks. I had quickly become impatient with my improvement and longed to be independent. The day I was able to stand in the shower was a major accomplishment for me.

After arriving home from the hospital, my daughter and husband initially had to help me undress and bathe. It was very humbling and often embarrassing for me to have my family see my scarred, bruised and frail body. They were so gracious and kind to me. I felt completely loved and cared for, and honestly I could not have performed basic care for myself. But, as time went on and I progressed in the healing process, I remember being elated at proposing the idea of bringing in a white resin patio chair I could sit in while showering, thereby relieving one of the assistants and providing me some privacy and independence. That worked well enough that I eventually improved to the point of standing in the shower with no chair.

The day it took only a half hour to put on a pair of jogging pants and sweatshirt was a day of victory and independence for me. I couldn't jog or sweat, but it felt amazing to accomplish that feat without help. I felt like my three-year-old granddaughter when I proclaimed, "I did it all by myself!"

I think God wants to see us persist in this life. He says, *"Let us run with perseverance the race marked out for us."* Hebrews 12:1

And He reminds us, *"You need to persevere so that when you have done the will of God, you will receive what he has promised."* Hebrews 10:36

We are not all in the same place spiritually, but as we press onward from glory to glory, we continue to see Him grow and mature us. Our small accomplishments are not small to God. Just as I wholeheartedly applauded my granddaughter for efforts and age-appropriate achievement, I believe God gets excited when we make even small strides. He certainly does not expect us all to be at the same stage in our Christian walk.

I often find it hard not to expect everyone around me to be where I am. I have actually self-diagnosed a problem I have become aware of over the past few years. Because I did not grow up in an emotionally healthy, wealthy, educated or professional family, I tend to think less of my potential and capabilities. I feel that if I know something, given my background and inadequacies, everyone else should know it as well. Consequently, if a person does not have the same knowledge or understanding that I have about something, I am easily frustrated with them. I can't imagine that they would not know something that I know.

Of course, that is wrong thinking because every achievement with the right heart and attitude is an ability given by God and we do not have the same strengths and gifts regardless of our experience. We should see our achievements as a gift from the Giver of Life and all good things. Rejoice in the steps leading to growth, perseverance and faith. Every stage of life has its own challenges and corresponding accomplishments.

Do not despise these small beginnings, for the LORD rejoices to see the work begin, to see the plumb line in Zerubbabel's hand.
Zechariah 4:10 (NLT)

KNOW SATISFACTION

But godliness with contentment is great gain. For we brought nothing into the world, and we can take nothing out of it. But if we have food and clothing, we will be content with that. 1 Timothy 6:6-8

When I was a small child, no more than nine years old, my great-grandmother had an auction one day, and it seemed as if everyone in our town came to the event. She lived in a small, white frame house in the city limits, in a neighborhood bordering a creek. The townspeople gathered around the home as my great-grandmother sat in a wooden chair outside the front door. She was a petite, thin woman with wrinkled skin and a hard-working, weathered appearance. Her sparse, stark-white, waist-length hair was always twisted like a pretzel on the back of her head. That day was the only time I ever saw grandma appear sad.

She was the kind of person who always had a pleasant smile on her petite face and seemed to enjoy life, regardless of her circumstances. She had lived long enough to see family and friends die. But that day, even though grandma didn't complain, she showed her sadness not on her face as much as in her nervousness. When grandma was frustrated or bored, she twiddled her thumbs. Lacing her boney fingers together, she would circle her thumbs clockwise and then counterclockwise.

She didn't grumble or protest, and it is only as I look back on the truth of what was happening that I realize what the day meant to her. She was parting with her possessions and her home, and later I learned that she was being moved to a nursing home. I watched people carry away dressers and wardrobes where her clothes had been stored. Surely they could smell the scent of her cologne as they loaded the heavy walnut furniture into their trucks. The pots, pans and dishes she had used during countless hours preparing meals for family and friends were now packed and carted away in crates and cardboard boxes. As the townspeople paraded their bargains in front of each other, grandma's thumbs twiddled all the more.

As a child, I remember being most impressed by seeing that many people in one place other than at school. I pestered my mom to let me play with some of the neighborhood kids in the creek. The highlight of my day was getting a blueberry snow-cone when the truck came around ringing its bell. The driver realized he had hit the jackpot at one stop as the sweltering heat drove customers to the white van boasting eight neon flavors of shaved ice. I'm sure the vendor made more money at that location than on the rest of the entire route, and maybe during the rest of the week. I don't remember if Grandma got a snow-cone that day, but she made the most of every day and every occasion.

After the auction, Grandma's worldly possessions went to other homes, some nearby and some far away. The new owners cooked with her pots and pans, slept in her bed, and fed their children from the kitchen table and chairs where I had once hidden with precision a mouthful of oatmeal under one of the seats.

As a child, I only thought of "what I got": a blueberry snow-cone from the vendor and a new friend from playing in the creek. At the end of the day, I was ready to go home. The blue evidence of the snow-cone remained around my mouth and tongue, my pant legs were damp, and my new friend's mother called her home for dinner. But at the end of the day, Grandma couldn't go into her house where she had lived for more than 50 years, because she no longer had a home. Many of her friends and family members were dead as she approached 92. Yet, she got into the car without a complaint or even a heavy sigh.

She spent the next few weeks at my grandmother's home and our house in the country. At night when she stayed at our house, she slept in a full-size bed between my sister and me and giggled like a school girl when we mimicked the screeching owls outside our window. We enjoyed pots of beef stew or fried chicken meals with handmade yeast rolls for dinner. She was eventually moved into a full-time nursing facility, and we visited often and brought her to our house for the weekends.

I learned a lot from that lady. She was never wealthy, but possessed much. She never complained while suffering more than her share of pain. She had very little education and yet was one of the wisest women I've ever met. What was the secret to her success? Like the apostle Paul, my great-grand-mother, Molly, had learned the mystery of contentment. They both would say, *"I have learned to be content whatever the circumstances. I know what it is to be in need, and I know what it is to have plenty. I have learned the secret of being content in any and every situation, whether well fed or hungry, whether living in plenty or in want."* Philippians 4:11-12

One of the key words in this verse is "learned." That tells me that contentment is not a natural response for most people, but that it can nevertheless be achieved. I've watched those who pattern their lives in such a way as to attain this "learned" contentment, rather than embracing a life of possessions, status and stuff. In this age of materialism, it's impossible not to be bitten at times by the green-eyed monster of selfishness and greed, and motivated to grasp for bigger, better and more. It's not only the "American way," but many countries are following our lead as we go down for the third time, drowning in our sea of trinkets and toys. And yet we are instructed in love to *"Keep your lives free from the love of money and be content with what you have, because God has said, 'Never will I leave you; never will I forsake you.'"* Hebrews 13:5

The fear of the Lord leads to life: Then one rests content, untouched by trouble.   Proverbs 19:23

TELL OTHERS
YOUR STORY

Much of our day is spent talking with family, friends and co-workers because we are certain they are interested in what we have to say and share. Even while standing in line at the post office or grocery store, we spend time exchanging words with strangers and clerks. I wonder how many times we realize that in doing this we are often giving a testimony. The definition of the word "testify" is 1) to make a factual statement based on personal experience or to declare something to be true from personal experience; 2) to be clear evidence of something; 3) to talk to an audience or group of listeners about personal experience as a Christian. (Wordweb Dictionary/Thesaurus)

It's not a term that we hear too much anymore. I can remember my mom going to our small country church one Wednesday evening for their prayer meeting. She came home and talked about the half dozen who had congregated and had given their testimonies. It was a voluntary, spontaneous time in the evening after a time of hymns when an individual would tell about what God was doing in their lives. Mom once told us about a gentleman who shared his testimony about God "cleaning up his mouth."

His story centered around his struggle to repair a bathroom leak in his home. He had been frustrated for days with the problem and after replacing the rusted pipe and tightening the nut, he turned on the water, expecting to enjoy a gentle flow of water through the pipes and a plumber's success. But, to his dismay, the water shot into his face, running down his beard and onto the floor; he felt his blood boil with anger. He said that he was tempted to take the wrench in his hand and "beat the sink off the wall" while a series of choice words came to his mind and approached his tongue.

The rotund, middle-aged gentleman rounded his broad shoulders as he sat in the oak church pew with his head in his rough hands and began to sob aloud. Some of the congregation had begun snickering mid-story from an uncomfortable nervousness, fearing the man's reputation might prompt him to share his crude language. But instead, he told how God had helped him to refrain from his natural tendencies and reactions. He shut off the water, grabbed a towel from the closet, first drying his face before mopping up the water, and began singing "Amazing Grace."

At that point in the prayer meeting, an elderly lady sitting adjacent to the man's pew started humming the chorus to the song. Within seconds the small group of attendees who had gathered on a sweltering summer night were lifting their voices to heaven declaring, "'Twas grace that brought me safe thus far and grace will lead me home." A simple man had been changed by God and wanted others to know. That was his testimony. We all have one.

When my daughters were growing up, I would remind them that no matter where they went or who they talked to, they were witnesses. Their words and actions would determine whether they were a good witness or a bad one. Either way, their witness mattered and had an affect on others.

Many people have said that they have been touched by

hearing my testimony of how God brought me back to life from certain death, and of the extraordinary story of God's healing power. But, just as I shared the story of the man proclaiming God's ability to rescue him from anger, that too is a miracle, not unlike mine, and upon sharing, it becomes a wonderful testimony.

There was a popular song several years ago, recorded by the contemporary Christian singing group Avalon. The chorus goes,

> For as long as I shall live,
> I will testify to love.
> I'll be a witness in the silences
> when words are not enough.
> With every breath I take
> I will give thanks to God above.
> For as long as I shall live,
> I will testify to love!

Tell your story.

TAKE OFF THE
GRAVE CLOTHES

... Jesus said, "If you hold to my teaching, you are really my disciples. Then you will know the truth, and the truth will set you free."   John 8:31-32

When I came to the place where I felt I was getting stronger and regaining some abilities, but still having problems, I wondered if I would ever fully recover. After being home for a few weeks, I became discouraged that I wasn't progressing as quickly as I had hoped. The magnitude of the head and foot injuries was greater than I had realized, and the implanted defibrillator in my chest seemed unbearable to live with. I could not believe the image in the mirror was my face and my body. I began to avoid my reflection, not even looking at myself when I brushed my teeth. I was sad and felt that I had lost my identity as a woman as well as my enthusiasm and purpose in life.

One morning as I was reading my Bible, I came to the story of Jesus raising Lazarus from the dead. It's a familiar story, and I had read the account many times, as well as commentaries about the New Testament incident.

Now Jesus, again sighing repeatedly and deeply disquieted, approached the tomb. It was a cave (a hole in the rock), and a boulder lay against [the entrance to close] it. Jesus said, "Take away the stone." Martha, the sister of the dead man, exclaimed, "But Lord, by this time he [is decaying and] throws off an offensive odor, for he has been dead four days!" Jesus said to her, "Did I not tell you and promise you that if you would believe and rely on Me, you would see the glory of God?" So they took away the stone. And Jesus lifted up His eyes and said, "Father, I thank You that You have heard Me. Yes, I know You always hear and listen to Me, but I have said this on account of and for the benefit of the people standing around, so that they may believe that You did send Me [that You have made Me Your Messenger]." When He had said this, He shouted with a loud voice, "Lazarus, come out!" And out walked the man who had been dead, his hands and feet wrapped in burial cloths (linen strips), and with a [burial] napkin bound around his face. Jesus said to them, "Free him of the burial wrappings and let him go."

John 11:38-44 (AMPLIFIED)

I thought about those verses for days after reading them. They continued to cause me to want to read and re-read the words to see what God was saying. I knew that I too had had an experience in which Jesus had literally raised my dead body, the day I collapsed on the floor at my workplace. In the hospital when I experienced an unknown fever and doctors continued to be amazed at my recovery; that was miraculous. Countless people prayed for me and rejoiced in God's goodness.

But after I came home from the hospital, I wasn't so sure I could or would fully recover. Even if my body continued to heal, I would be left with scars. And, even if I returned to work and other activities, would I ever go into the kitchen at work where I had collapsed or go to bed without dread or fear? Yes, I was alive, and I thanked God several times a day. But shouldn't there be more?

My mind wandered, and then I was drawn back to the page. When I read the words, *"And out walked the man who had been dead, his hands and feet wrapped in burial cloths and with a napkin bound around his face. Jesus said to them, 'Free him of the burial wrappings and let him go.'"* I wondered what, if anything, did that passage have to do with me?

The first thing I noticed was the idea that Lazarus was a walking dead man until those bindings were removed. I could easily relate that to how I felt. I saw myself as a person who had been "raised from the dead," but who was somehow unable or unwilling to remove the hindrances that continued to discourage and defeat me. I also saw that the passage referred to "others" removing the wrappings.

Unfortunately, sometimes, well-meaning friends and family members can be a hindrance to our freedom in Christ. They know us best – our past mistakes, weaknesses and failures. They predict what might happen and unintentionally hinder our progress, because they truly want to protect us from danger or embarrassment. In reality, they can make it difficult for us to move beyond the past and press forward. I think often they fear that change may require them to rethink their own lives.

So, while the familiar appears to be safe, we have to listen for godly direction as we change and grow. Jesus spoke to Lazarus' family and friends, instructing them to remove his grave clothes, and He will do the same for our good. Of course, we are the ones most responsible for clinging to and dragging around the grave clothes. Initially, Lazarus had to personally respond to Jesus' call to rise from his sleep, step out of the tomb, and walk into the light. I suppose he could have refused to respond and could have remained in the burial place. After all, the dead man's body had been there for four days.

I know even when I've had the flu or short illness, my body quickly regresses and it becomes more difficult with each day to become mobile and motivated. Plus, the longer we delay a response, the less likely we are to do or change anything. So, when Lazarus heard the call to "come out," he had to follow Jesus' voice, trusting Him with each step.

I began to see myself in the passage. Personally, even though I had been resuscitated and my body revived, I was still restrained by lifeless thoughts and worthless goals and ambitions. I didn't struggle with drugs, alcohol, infidelity or materialism. I respected authority, paid my taxes and loved my family. But, because I continue to live in this mortal, imperfect body, I struggle just as everyone does. I want to be "healthy, wealthy and wise," as Benjamin Franklin's *Poor Richard's Almanac* says. Society tells us that if we're not young, beautiful, rich and adored by thousands of fans, we have failed in this life. The never-ending whirlwind of self-image and the need for approval keeps us running in circles, chasing the wind, unfulfilled.

Maybe the story is too familiar. We've heard it, we've seen it and we eventually experience it ourselves. Lazarus was bound hands, feet and head after he emerged from the tomb. That affected everything: what he did, where he went, and how he thought. What benefit would it have been for the man to be raised from the dead, but unable to function in life? Sin and this world affect us all, but we do not have to be "bound" by thoughts and ideas. We have to choose to "come out" and "take off the grave clothes."

Jesus replied, "I tell you the truth, everyone who sins is a slave to sin. Now a slave has no permanent place in the family, but a son belongs to it forever. So if the Son sets you free, you will be free indeed."   John 8:34-36

DEO VOLENTE –
GOD WILLING

All of our plans should begin and end with the Latin phrase, *Deo volente*, meaning, "God willing."

Now listen, you who say, "Today or tomorrow we will go to this or that city, spend a year there, carry on business and make money." Why, you do not even know what will happen tomorrow. What is your life? You are a mist that appears for a little while and then vanishes. Instead, you ought to say, "If it is the Lord's will, we will live and do this or that." As it is, you boast and brag. All such boasting is evil.   James 4:13-16

I think most of us are guilty of planning our lives to the extreme for our future and our children. Sure, we are told to save for the future, count the cost before beginning a project, invest in others, and be wise planners as in the parable of the five wise and five foolish virgins who trimmed their lamps in preparation for the bridegroom. Without planning, we would otherwise find ourselves without direction and purpose, and neglecting the work God has in store for us. It's when we need to control and manipulate every situation that we forget that we are not in charge – God is.

And He (Jesus) told them a parable, saying, "The land of a rich man was very productive. And he began reasoning to himself, saying, 'What shall I do, since I have no place to store my crops?' Then he said, 'This is what I will do: I will tear down my barns and build larger ones, and there I will store all my grain and my goods. And I will say to my soul, "Soul, you have many goods laid up for many years to come; take your ease, eat, drink and be merry."' But God said to him, 'You fool! This very night your soul is required of you; and now who will own what you have prepared?' So is the man who stores up treasure for himself, and is not rich toward God." Luke 12:16-21 (NASB)

The day I collapsed at work, I not only had my day planned, but I knew what I was having for lunch and dinner, the staff and clients I would be meeting with that day, and my schedule for the entire week. My family was planning for our annual pre-Christmas vacation to Orlando and gearing up for a Chuck E. Cheese celebration with our granddaughter over the weekend. It was life as usual – busy, busy, busy.

But, the moment my heart stopped pumping blood to my brain and body, the entire agenda ended and my plans ceased. The things that had been so important for me to do suddenly didn't matter. No one around me cared about the non-essentials, and I certainly didn't either. I wasn't concerned with my clothing and accessories, as my business attire was quickly removed in exchange for a hospital gown. The new haircut that I had gotten the night before turned out to be a total waste of time and money.

After a long day at work, I had spent three hours and $80 at the salon only to have it half shaved and lying on the operating room floor. Amazingly, not one of the neurosurgeons or nurses was aghast and not one of them was more interested in my hair than my bleeding brain. The phone calls and emails that needed to be answered and addressed were forgotten. My independence was limited; I wasn't able to feed, bathe or dress myself for a period of time and was unable to drive a vehicle for six months, a time during which my husband graciously became my chauffeur.

Even following the four months after my hospitalization, my job was reduced from a 40-50 hour workweek as fulltime director of an entire department managing several staff and being responsible for volunteers, programs and clients to a part-time program coordinator's position. Packing personal photos and memorabilia, I moved a few necessities from my private office to a shared workspace. Even though I had been a capable manager in the past, I felt that my staff viewed me differently, with less confidence and administration appeared overly concerned that I might "collapse" under the pressure. So literally everything changed.

At the risk of seeming to throw myself a pity party and being the lone attendee, I'm simply sharing my experience of how plans can be interrupted in a heartbeat (or in my case, the lack of one). I think we often believe life is a never-ending series of ups and downs or highs and lows, but there is nothing that can't be worked out, worked through or worked into our agenda. The day I left my house for work on October 14th, I didn't consider that I would not be back home that evening to eat dinner with my family, discuss the evening news and weather or sleep in my bed. If I had known I would not be coming back for weeks or not at all, I'm sure that Wednesday would have been very different.

I would have told my daughter how proud I was of her and how contagious her laughter and enthusiasm for life are to me. I would have hugged my granddaughter while stroking her long golden hair and told her that she is a precious gift from God and that I love watching her grow even though it has gone too quickly.

I would have taken time to enjoy a large bacon and egg breakfast while sipping on orange juice with lots of pulp in a stemmed glass. I would have spent time in prayer for my mom and dad as they struggle with her Alzheimer's disease and for my older daughter, who was so far away from everything and everyone she has known. And, before I walked out the garage door to my car, I would have looked into my husband's deep brown eyes and told him how much I need him and love him. I would have lost the attitude but expressed my gratitude for his commitment to and sacrificial love for me and our girls, and how much richer my life has been because of him.

But I didn't do any of those things that day. I didn't give the day a second thought. Oh sure, I had plans and expectations for the next 12 hours – places to go, things to do, people to see. And, then literally, in the blink of an eye, it was gone. All of my plans, ideas, dreams and expectations were gone and in the past. All the things I had wanted to do or hoped to say were suddenly missed opportunities.

People have often asked me if I saw a bright light, a glimpse of heaven or heard a special word from God. I wish I had; I'm sure I would have been asked to appear on popular TV talk shows and could have sold a lot more books. But, the truth is, I don't remember much of anything while I was waiting for God to bring me back to life. The truth is, if I hadn't been resuscitated, I'm certain the angels would have escorted me to my new home and I would have dined with royalty that evening.

But, the reality of life after sudden death came to me in a slower and more practical way. My "revelation" didn't appear as quickly as the cardiac arrest. It has been much as in that favorite scene in the "Wizard of Oz," in which the good witch Glinda tells Dorothy that she could have returned home at any time in her experience but the lesson that she had to learn was the key. Her lesson was simple. Mine appears to be just as simple, but also involves a more lengthy process (probably because I wasn't wearing ruby slippers).

Dorothy learned that if she ever went looking for her heart's desire she wouldn't look any farther than her own back yard, "because if it isn't there, I never really lost it to begin with." In other words, learn to be happy with what you have and where you are. Beyond that, enjoy, embrace, be thankful for the life God has given you.

For Dorothy Gale, the lesson she learned was that life could be worse than living on the farm with Aunt Em and Uncle Henry. For me, many of the lessons I've shared in these pages are an ongoing process, not an overnight change or a light-bulb experience or sudden awareness. I have had a few "revelations," and God has given me insight into some areas of my life.

Seven months after the hospitalization and recovery, I made my way back to Springfield Lake. I had the day off work, so after dropping off my granddaughter at preschool, I decided to take a short hike to the top of a bluff I was familiar with. I had only been permitted to drive for the past month, so anytime I got behind the wheel of the car, I felt like a teenager with a new driver's license.

At first, I used the gas pedal with caution, adjusted my mirrors and seat position and came to a full stop at the end of our rural cul-de-sac. Quickly gaining confidence, I turned up the volume on the stereo and opened the sunroof. Almost giddy, I openly smiled and sang along with the music. I had forgotten the feeling of freedom that driving gives a person.

But this particular day, I just needed some time to myself, to think and process things, without a well-meaning, compassionate, concerned audience inquiring about my physical state. The short drive provided a sense of liberty and the lake always proved to be a visual reminder of God's majesty and beauty.

I took my time climbing the trail leading to the bluff overlooking the water. I sat down and caught my breath, remembering that it is healthy to have a reaction to physical exertion. I lingered at the sight before me and took it all in. The deep, aqua pool of water rippled as the wind toyed with it and caused a fish to leap for joy. Geese flew overhead in a perfect V formation, chattering and honking as they chose a suitable landing site. The breeze brushed my cheek and hair; I actually had hair long enough to be disheveled!

I began praising God for all the things my eyes, mind and spirit were experiencing. As a farm girl, I have always responded to nature in a way that provides a calmness and tranquility. It helps me relate to the obvious provisions from God to His creation. And, I am quickly reminded that He says, *"Do not worry about your life, what you will eat or drink; or about your body, what you will wear. Is not life more important than food, and the body more important than clothes? Look at the birds of the air; they do not sow or reap or store away in barns, and yet your heavenly Father feeds them. Are you not much more valuable than they? Who of you by worrying can add a single hour to his life? Therefore do not worry about tomorrow, for tomorrow will worry about itself. Each day has enough trouble of its own."*

Matthew 6:25-27, 34

That morning, I was worrying. After all, if God had spared my life (again), He must have a very good reason, and I had set out to get my assignment. I was willing to do anything to show Him how much I loved Him and wanted to serve Him. After a time in wide-eyed prayer, I asked, "Lord, why did you save my life?"

When I experienced the heart problem after the birth of my second child and God allowed me to live, I was convinced that I was on this earth to care for my children and provide a godly home where they would feel loved and nurtured. After my children grew up, graduated from high school and then college, I wondered if my days were numbered and racing near the end, since I had fulfilled my purpose. I kept finding reasons God needed me here, but now I struggled with knowing why He chose to keep me here. I confessed that I had made a mess out of several areas of life and prepared myself to hear that God had me here to minister or serve someone else; in essence, "it's not about you."

But as the wind whipped the waves and the sun danced on the water, a seemingly quiet, still voice spoke, not into my ear, but to my heart. "I did it for **you**," He said. "I preserved your life for **you** because I love **you**. It's my gift – enjoy it."

He wasn't asking for anything from me in return. He wasn't expecting me to try to repay Him (not that I could). I could not believe how long I had struggled to please Him with works, even though I knew my salvation does not come through any efforts of my own. However, my love language is "acts of service," and naturally when I care for someone, I show them by doing something for them. I have tried to serve my family, friends, church and community, partially as an offering to God.

I never felt that what I did was enough or good enough, but God continued to give me chances so others could experience His goodness through my acts of services. I realized at that moment that God not only loved me enough to send His Son to die for me, but He loved me enough to give me life, not only eternal life (as amazing as that is), but real, abundant life, here and now, and forever.

Clearly, God is not finished with me, which is evidenced by the fact that I have survived two cardiac arrests and other life-threatening obstacles. Also, He hasn't allowed me to be here just because someone else couldn't do my job at work, prepare meals and care for my family, write books or take photos. I'm certain that God could have gotten several candidates for those positions, but I believe He heard the prayers of my family and friends and chose to leave me here to fulfill His good pleasure and purpose. I would have left that statement as the sum total of my reason for remaining alive. But, now I also know that I am alive because God loves me and wants me to enjoy the life He has given... to me.

Honestly, there is something that no one else can do as well as I can; no one can tell my story and glorify Him the way I can. I didn't say "better," but without hesitation, I know that no one has my testimony of His goodness and grace to me. Just as no one has your testimony. No one can tell your story because it is as personal as your relationship to Him.

Because of my incident, I don't take anything about my heart for granted: the physical, emotional or spiritual. That rhythmic beating muscle is music to my ears; it's only when it skips a beat or pounds in my chest that I become a little anxious. Without the ability of that significant organ to circulate blood and oxygen, none of us can continue life in these bodies.

Emotionally, hearts are broken but likewise, often comforted. Spiritually, the heart is "desperately wicked" but conversely is made alive and quickened by the Spirit at the moment of salvation. We hear from the first time we attend church or Sunday School that we must "give our hearts to Jesus." A fetus first hears his mother's heartbeat as it develops and grows, later being comforted as a baby at her breast.

Mostly, what I've become increasingly aware of is that I

constantly have a thankful heart. I see things as I've never seen them, with appreciation and awe. I hear sounds I've never heard, from the whisper of the wind and the soothing ripples of a stream to the power of rumbling thunder in the distance. Suddenly I can enjoy and savor food for its unique flavor, texture and the cook's signature. Tasks are an opportunity to serve and enjoy the satisfaction that work brings. Family is a precious gift of joy, acceptance and commitment next to God.

God has allowed me to live for Him and I continue to learn, grow and share my experience and His goodness with others. I hope I will never again take my life for granted, forgetting the gift and more importantly, the Giver. I pray that you will embrace life and enjoy the days ahead.

If you read the pages of this book and find yourself feeling uncomfortable about life and death issues, I encourage you to do three things – resist fear, find real hope and truth in the Bible, and live every day on this earth to the fullest. God does not want us to be ignorant about our lives and His plans. He has provided life eternal that does not begin at the time of death, but begins the moment you choose Jesus Christ as your Savior to take the death penalty handed down to every person.

For all have sinned and fall short of the glory of *God.*   Romans 3:23

He is not hiding that information, but wants you to seek and find the life He has for you.

For the Son of Man came to seek and to save what was lost. Luke 19:10

Without faith it is impossible to please God, because anyone who comes to him must believe that he exists and that he rewards those who earnestly seek him. Hebrews 11:6

Take your Bible and begin reading the New Testament book of John followed by Romans. As the spirit of God leads you, talk to Him, not withholding anything. Your life will never be the same and you will embark on a journey that begins in this life and continues forever.

IN CLOSING...

The following verses are my favorites, and I have often drawn comfort and encouragement from them. Ask God to use these or any other verse in the Bible He chooses to speak personally to you and your situation. Write the date next to the verse and be reminded of His faithfulness time and time again. Hold onto His Word and expect Him to be near, no matter where you find yourself.

Do you not know? Have you not heard?
The LORD is the everlasting God,
 the Creator of the ends of the earth.
He will not grow tired or weary,
 and his understanding no one can fathom.
He gives strength to the weary and increases
 the power of the weak.
Even youths grow tired and weary,
 and young men stumble and fall;
But those who hope in the LORD
 will renew their strength.
They will soar on wings like eagles;
 they will run and not grow weary,
 they will walk and not be faint.

Isaiah 40:28-31

When you pass through the waters,
* I will be with you;*
And when you pass through the rivers,
* they will not sweep over you.*
When you walk through the fire,
* you will not be burned;*
* the flames will not set you ablaze.*

Isaiah 43:2

Surely the arm of the LORD
* is not too short to save, nor his ear*
* too dull to hear.*

Isaiah 59:1

Teach me your way, O LORD,
* and I will walk in your truth;*
Give me an undivided heart,
* that I may fear your name.*
I will praise you, O Lord my God,
* with all my heart;*
I will glorify your name forever.
For great is your love toward me;
* you have delivered me*
* from the depths of the grave.*

Psalm 86:11-13

For inquiries about *Rhythms of the Heart*, to order copies of the book, or to schedule a speaking engagement with Debra Tucker, email: rhythmsoftheheart10@gmail.com